From
ORPHANS
to
HEIRS

Published by
The Bible Reading Fellowship
Peter's Way, Sandy Lane West
Oxford OX4 5HG
ISBN 1 84101 023 5

First published 1999
10 9 8 7 6 5 4 3 2 1 0

Acknowledgments
Unless otherwise stated, scripture quotations are taken
from *The Holy Bible, New International Version*, copyright
© 1973, 1978, 1984 by International Bible Society.
Used by permission of Hodder & Stoughton Limited. All
rights reserved. 'NIV' is a registered trademark of
International Bible Society. UK trademark number
1448790

A catalogue record for this book is available from the
British Library

Printed and bound in Great Britain by
Caledonian Book Manufacturing International, Glasgow

From
ORPHANS
to
HEIRS

Celebrating our spiritual adoption

Mark Stibbe

This book is dedicated to my mother,
Joy Stibbe

THE FATHER'S SMILE

PHILIP STIBBE

ACKNOWLEDGMENTS

Many thanks, Naomi Starkey, for encouraging me to write this book, and for your patience with me when promised deadlines were not met.

Many thanks to all of you at St Andrew's, for your feedback when I presented the material of this book in the form of a sermon series during the autumn of 1998.

Many thanks, Amanda Lee and Michael McCrum, for reading the manuscript, for making invaluable suggestions, and for spotting a number of things that needed correcting.

Many thanks to Keith Hubbard for your help behind the scenes with identifying some of the vital academic studies in the field.

Many thanks, R.T., not only for the wonderful foreword you've written to this book, but also for your initial enthusiasm and for your continuing friendship—which is very highly valued.

Many thanks, Alie, for all your patience with me when I've been so focused on this book that I've not given you or the children the time you've deserved.

Many thanks, Lord, for the inspiration you've given during the writing of this book. The good things are all yours, the errors are of course all mine!

CONTENTS

FOREWORD

The time is long overdue that the church generally should rediscover the New Testament teaching of adoption. When you read this book, you will see for yourself why I say this. You may well ask, 'Where have I been all my life?' It is astonishing that such a clear and comforting teaching could be buried so deeply in the theological archives of church history.

To put it another way, when you grasp this teaching of adoption you see that, by being adopted into God's family, you get everything that was given to Christ—God's only 'natural' Son, if I may put it that way. Martin Luther turned the world upside down by his rediscovery of justification by faith alone. But with being adopted, you get that justification thrown in as well. John Calvin articulated the doctrines of the sovereignty of God. But with adoption, that too is thrown in, for only God does the choosing and the keeping of those he adopted.

This is a wonderful book. It may be that this will be the instrument by which the teaching of adoption is given the high profile it deserves alongside those aforementioned doctrines that emerged so ostensibly in the sixteenth century. Perhaps the delay awaited a man like Dr Mark Stibbe who could draw on both his personal background and biblical expertise.

If anything is needed as much as the remarriage of the Word and the Spirit, in a day when the two are sadly so separated and even polarized, it is fresh scholarship that is mirrored by the combination of the Word and the Spirit. Dr Stibbe reflects that quality of scholarship. For when it comes to those who are academics nowadays, precious few have a clue as to the things of the Holy Spirit. And I have to say that when it comes to those who are enamoured with the Holy Spirit, it is not very easy to find those who are at home with serious and competent scholarship. Dr Stibbe is one of those exceptions.

You will be thrilled as you read this book. I dare say, you are probably not prepared for it. You will weep with joy again and again. I cannot repeat that story of the painting of the art collector's son without coming to tears.

I pray for every reader, that you will be blessed beyond your greatest expectations as you enter into brilliantly green pastures.

R. T. Kendall
Westminster Chapel, London, 1999

COMMENDATIONS

We live today... in an almost fatherless society... The good news, however, is that God is the Father of the fatherless. Mark's book is powerful in helping to understand that the grace of God alone brings freedom. Indeed, the freedom to journey 'from orphans to heirs'.

Mark is well able to help those in slavery make the journey. Not only is he a gifted pastor, teacher, prophet, and revivalist but he himself was an orphan—one unwanted and disowned. His writing comes not only out of good biblical theology, but, as importantly, out of a life of experiencing God's adoptive grace. As a minister and also a friend of Mark, I not only heartily recommend this book to everyone. I also want to state that Mark lives by a standard of freedom characterized by the defining quote of the book: 'A true Christian is therefore not a person who is driven by whips but drawn by cords of love'.

Marc A. Dupont, Mantle of Praise Ministries, Ft Wayne, Indiana, USA

Mark Stibbe's latest book is a powerful blend of scholarship, personal experience and pastoral awareness. It restores the theme of adoption to its rightful place in our thinking and does so vividly and effectively. This is a book for pastors and people and is well worth the asking price.

Dr Nigel Wright, Senior Pastor, Altrincham Baptist Church

This book arises out of teaching that I heard Mark give at St Andrew's Church, Chorleywood. It is truly a life-changing message. I saw many deeply affected and radically transformed as a result of this series on spiritual adoption. As one of those greatly helped by this teaching, I can unreservedly recommend this book. It is destined to become a spiritual classic for the 21st-century church.

J. John, international evangelist

If ever there was a book for our times, this is it! The great biblical truth of our adoption as God's children is here brought to light. *From Orphans to Heirs* is full of insights which inform the mind and warm the heart—a must for this fatherless generation.

Mike Pilavachi, leader of Soul Survivor, Watford

STAY

Will you hold me in your arms
As I rest on your knee?
Won't you tell me my favourite story?
I was an orphan,
You adopted me.

As I listen to your voice the blessing surrounds me.
I know I am yours,
I'm so glad you found me;
I was an orphan,
You adopted me.

As I look in your eyes
I see such kindness;
Nothing in the world is anything like this.
I was an orphan,
You adopted me.

Chorus:

Wrap your strong arms around me,
This is my peace.
Father, stay close by me,
Stay . . .

BRIAN DOERKSEN

A BRIEF APOLOGY

Before I begin, I just want to say sorry to those readers who are offended by exclusive rather than inclusive language. I appreciate that there are probably some who will be upset by my constant references to the journey from slavery to 'sonship', on the grounds that it sounds as if it excludes women. Let me say right at the outset that this is not my intention at all. The Bible chooses to use the language of sonship about the status of all believers, women as well as men. In doing this there is never any suggestion that this does not include women or girls. 'Sonship', 'sons', and other related words are always inclusive of both sexes when they apply to our position as the adopted children of God.

There are three reasons why I have not sought to be more inclusive in my use of language. The first is because there is something catchy in the alliterative phrase, 'slavery to sonship'. I know this is a rather feeble reason but it has been a factor. Secondly, it would have overloaded the book terribly if I had put 'daughterhood' every time I had to write 'sonship', and 'daughters' every time I had to write 'sons'. I have done this from time to time in order to remind the reader that I mean both women and men when I speak about 'sonship'. Thirdly, in the world of the New Testament it was the son who inherited the father's estate. There is therefore a cultural reason for the biblical use of 'sonship' in connection with the idea of inheritance. Although this is not the case in many cultures today, it was a fact of life then, so I have usually left talk of 'sons' unchanged.

In the final analysis, I hope and pray that my use of language will not be interpreted to mean that adoption is a privilege for 'men only'.

CHAPTER 1

The Lost Coin

Jesus once told a parable about a lost coin (Luke 15:8–9). It's one of the shortest of his stories and yet it has great significance.

Once upon a time, a woman possessed ten coins. One day, she lost one of the ten. Out of an intense desire to recover it, she then lit a lamp, swept the entire house, and searched carefully until she eventually found it again. As soon as she recovered it, she called her friends and neighbours together and asked them to celebrate with her. All the effort had been worthwhile. Therefore, it was time to have a party.
(MY PARAPHRASE)

Now obviously, in its original context, this little parable is all about lost souls. The chapter as a whole focuses on the lost:

1 The Lost Sheep (vv. 1–7)
2 The Lost Coin (vv. 8–10)
3 The Lost Son (vv. 11–32)

The point Jesus is making in each of these stories is this: God is passionate and intentional about pursuing lost people. He is deeply concerned to go after sinners and to bring them home into his arms of love. Each of these stories reveals the Father's heart for those who do not yet know him. We shall be looking closely at the third of these stories in Chapter 6.

At the same time, the parable of the lost coin speaks to me of something lost to Christian believers over the centuries. I see the woman in the story as an illustration of the Christian church. She has a supply of precious coins, stored away. These coins I liken to the major traditional doctrines of Christian theology. They are like deposits of theological truth given in scripture and then elaborated into statements of faith throughout the centuries. We might see these ten coins as the following:

1 The Doctrine of God and Creation
2 The Doctrine of Christ and the Spirit
3 The Doctrine of the Trinity
4 The Doctrine of Man
5 The Doctrine of Justification
6 The Doctrine of Adoption
7 The Doctrine of Sanctification
8 The Doctrine of the Word of God
9 The Doctrine of the Future
10 The Doctrine of the Church

Since the time of the earliest church, these doctrines have been discussed and developed. All, that is, except one. One of these coins has been lost to the church. One of them has received little attention, to the great detriment of believers and the great impoverishment of the church as a whole. As you look at the list, I wonder whether you have spotted the lost coin.

A NEGLECTED TREASURE

For me, the lost coin is the doctrine of spiritual adoption. Of all the ten great doctrines, this is the one that has been lost under the carpet and neglected for nearly two thousand years of church history.

Martin Luther, who rediscovered the great truth that we are justified by faith, did the church a great service. He led people to focus on what Jim Packer calls 'the foundational blessing of the gospel'[1]—that we are made righteous before a holy God by believing that sin's price has been paid in full on the cross. By believing that Jesus died for my sins, I can say today that it is 'Just as if I'd never sinned!' I can say, 'I'm justified!'

Unfortunately, this same emphasis on justification led to the neglect of what Packer calls 'the highest blessing of the Gospel'[2]—that we are adopted as sons and daughters of our heavenly Father through the work of the Holy Spirit. Subsequently, churches have been encouraged to concentrate on the finished work of the cross (justification), but not on the continuing work of the Spirit (adoption). As a result, the doctrine of spiritual adoption has traditionally been turned into a short postscript in what is seen as the far weightier truth of justification by faith. As one biblical scholar has put it:

In spite of its importance adoption has failed generally to gain much prominence in the great treatments of systematic and biblical theology. Its discussion frequently ended with an investigation of its relation to regeneration, justification, and sanctification. Consequently it was treated as a minor aspect of the way of salvation.[3]

Why has the doctrine of spiritual adoption been so neglected? There are three main reasons. The first has to do with the scarcity of any actual *experience* of what John Wesley called 'the loving spirit of adoption' in church history. Such a lack of authentic charismatic experience has had disastrous consequences. Theologians dominated by a Greek rather than a Hebraic way of thinking have, over the centuries, cultivated a religion of the head rather than the heart. As A.W. Tozer once put it:

The experiential heart theology of a grand army of fragrant saints is rejected in favour of a smug interpretation of Scripture which would have sounded strange to an Augustine, a Rutherford or a Brainerd.[4]

What an amazing statement that is! Over the centuries, many of the great teachers of the church have produced a theology that has brought light to the head but not heat to the heart. It is this tragic lack of what Tozer calls an 'experiential heart theology' that lies behind the neglect of the doctrine of spiritual adoption. In other words, a lack of openness to the actual experience of the Holy Spirit has led to a widespread ignorance concerning the joy, liberty and intimacy of adopted sonship. Only during times of revival will you find any rigorous teaching about spiritual adoption. Thus it is people like Jonathan Edwards, John Wesley and Charles Spurgeon who preach and write about adoption, and they do that first and foremost because they *experienced* the 'loving spirit of adoption'[5] during seasons of the Spirit.

The second reason has to do with the church's difficulties concerning predestination and free will. At this point I want to own up to my own personal investment in this book. You see, I am an adopted child. My twin sister and I spent our first few months in an orphanage in Hackney, North London. When we were adopted, Philip and Joy Stibbe took us out of that orphanage and brought us home to live with them. When all this happened, the truth of the matter is that Philip (and my mother Joy) chose us. We did not choose them (we were only infants, after all!)

When God adopted us into his family the Bible says that he 'predestined us to be adopted as his sons' and that this divine choice took place 'before the creation of the world' (Ephesians 1:4–6). In other words, the Father decided in advance that he would adopt us. He made up his mind before the foundation of the universe that he would choose some of us out of the orphanage of this world to be his sons and daughters. If you are a Christian—born again by the Spirit of God—then that is because the Father chose you to be his child. He decided that he wanted you in his family before he flung the stars into space. What a great privilege that is!

At the same time, there is an apparent down side to this truth. For many there is something rather scandalous about God choosing some and not choosing others to be adopted as his sons and daughters. It is this nervous apprehension over the doctrine of predestination that has, I believe, contributed towards the neglect of our spiritual adoption. For a great number of people, the notion of 'supernatural selection' seems as ruthless as Darwin's idea of 'natural selection'.

A third reason why the doctrine of adoption has been something of a lost coin is because our translations of the Bible have often concealed this truth from us. Recently I spoke to a group of Swedish students in Stockholm. My subject was spiritual adoption. I took them through the five New Testament passages where the word 'adoption' occurs. In every case, their Swedish translations had failed to render the Greek word *huiothesia* as 'adoption'. For this reason alone the doctrine of spiritual adoption was new to them.

Even some of our English translations are guilty of obscuring the great glory of spiritual adoption. The New International Version (NIV) translates Romans 8:15 as follows: 'For you did not receive a spirit that makes you a slave again to fear but you received the Spirit of sonship'. The word translated 'sonship' is the Greek word *huiothesia*, meaning adoption. Here is the NIV translation of Galatians 4:5–6: 'But when the time had fully come, God sent his Son, born of a woman, born under law, to redeem those under law, that we might receive the full rights of sons'. The phrase 'full rights of sons' is a translation of *huiothesia*, which most recent researchers insist should be translated 'adoption'.[6] In translating *huiothesia* as 'sonship' rather than the more accurate and accessible word 'adoption', some of our versions of the Bible have unwittingly contributed to the demise of this particular doctrine in the church.

Here then are three reasons why the church has left the lost coin under the carpet. The first has to do with our resistance to the experience of the fire of the Father's love. The second has to do with our tendency to shy away from anything that smacks of predestination. The third has to do with inadequate translations of the word *huiothesia*. During the course of this book I am going to question these three issues. My thesis is that the doctrine of adoption needs to be restored to a place of honour among the great truths of the church. When you consider that there are five places in Paul's letters alone where the word *huiothesia* is used, it seems extraordinary that this should need to be said. There are only two passages where being 'born again' is mentioned, yet no Bible-believing Christian questions the importance of regeneration!

I firmly believe that it is time for the church to use the light of the Spirit's revelation, to sweep through God's word and to search diligently for the lost coin of spiritual adoption. Without this doctrine, we will always be incompletely initiated into the kingdom of God. We will enjoy the foundational blessing of the gospel without experiencing its highest blessing. We will believe that we are born again and that we are children of God, but we will lack the actual experience of sonship and daughterhood that enables us to cultivate a lifelong relationship of intimacy with our Father in heaven. This should not be allowed to go on any longer, otherwise there will always be a tendency for us to live as slaves rather than sons.

In the remainder of this first chapter I would like to offer you three reasons why it is essential for all believers to understand and experience the 'loving spirit of adoption':

It enriches our image of God

I don't know what your image of God is, but I can say this with some confidence—many believers never move on from an image of God as a punitive judge. When I was converted at the age of seventeen, I asked Jesus Christ to come into my life to be my Saviour. I did this primarily because a quiet voice inside my heart had said, 'Mark Stibbe, if you died tonight, where would you stand before the judgment seat of Christ?' I realized at that moment that I was a sinner, that I was in desperate danger while I was outside the boundaries of God's love, and that there was a great urgency to repent.

What happened next is recorded in my book, *Thinking Clearly About Revival.*[7] However, what I didn't say there was that my image of God for the first few years of my Christian life was that he was a stern judge, not a loving father. I was taught to fear God, but not to love him. The net result of this was that I started to live a life of legalism rather than a life of love. However hard I tried, I couldn't live up to God's standards. I functioned as a slave rather than as a son. The main reason was because of a deficient image of God.

Many people suffer from this and indeed some never escape from it. If we are to be set free we must move from a place where we fear God to a place where we can love him as well. For this to occur, we must allow the Holy Spirit to flood our hearts with the revelation of God as 'Abba, Father'. In other words, we need the loving spirit of adoption to penetrate the deepest places of our lives and to bring about a divine disclosure of the true nature of God. In short, we need to move from slavery to sonship.

Once upon a time, a couple wanted to adopt a child. After careful research, an adoption society gave them the name of a child who might be suitable. The backgrounds of both the child and the adopting parents were then carefully checked before the child was brought to their home to see if he felt comfortable with the prospective parents. At the end of that trial period, they were all assessed for suitability and then invited to a local courtroom.

The adopting parents sat in the courtroom looking up at the judge on his platform. He looked at them with the sternest expression and spoke in the gravest tones.

'I have not yet signed my name on this certificate of adoption. Up until now you have had a choice whether to say yes or whether to say no to this child. If I sign this piece of paper, then this child will be yours for ever. There will be no going back. According to the law of this state, it will be as if he is your natural son. Now you don't have any idea how he is going to turn out. He could turn to drugs. He could cost you everything. Now consider. Do you want me to sign this certificate?'

The adopting parents said, 'Yes.'

At this moment, the judge came down from the platform and, with tears in his eyes, handed them the signed certificate. He looked at them and said, 'You have made a wonderful decision, and I can say that with certainty because I too have an adopted son.'

Did you see what happened in that story? The judge came down from the high, intimidating and remote place, stepped forward and revealed himself as a loving, adopting father!

Now I submit to you that many Christians still live with a picture of God as a stern judge who speaks in grave tones. Consequently, the whole of their Christian lives is spent in the courtroom. Every morning they dutifully have their quiet times, but these times are spent in the dock dealing with the gnawing guilt of having failed in ways both small and great.

If you are such a person, then you need to have a revelation of God as he truly is. You need to see him step down from that remote place and disclose himself as a 'dad'. Once that happens, you will no longer be a slave but a son or a daughter. You will no longer be in the courtroom with a judge, you'll be in the living-room with the Father. Oh yes, you will still have a holy fear of God. But more than anything, you will know him as a Father who is passionate about intimacy with you, and this truth will become the basis for everything you are and do.

It enriches our experience of God

This is the second reason why we so desperately need a better grasp of our adoption. It is at this point that I want to return to a point I made earlier about the neglect of the experiential dimension to Christianity. The truth is that there are many believers who have a dutiful relationship with God based on the scriptures, but there are not so many who have a joyful relationship with him based on the Spirit. Indeed, there are even fewer who are men and women of both the word and the Spirit, of doctrine and experience, scripture and the power of God (Matthew 22:29).

A few months ago I went to one of our St Andrew's satellite churches to bless the handing on of the leadership from a couple called George and Margaret to a younger couple, Martin and Judy. After the morning service, Martin handed George and Margaret a certificate of adoption. On this piece of paper, which he had designed himself, Martin stipulated that George and Margaret were now adopted as parents. From this moment on, George and Margaret were to be treated as members of Martin and Judy's family.

Not surprisingly, the certificate of adoption caught my attention and I mentioned after the service to Martin that it would be wonderful to have a certificate of spiritual adoption to hand to those who had come to know God as Father during my sermon series on slavery and sonship (a series that forms the backbone of this book). He said that he would design one, and we have been using it ever since.

That same evening at St Andrew's a number of us met before the 6.15pm service in order to seek the Lord and to ask him to reveal his plans and desires for the meeting. At the very end of this time, a young man (who had not been present at the morning events) gave this word: 'There is someone here tonight who is going to receive their certificate of spiritual adoption.' As he said this, my eyes opened, George nearly fell off his seat, and Margaret and I looked at each other with excitement.

At the conclusion of the service, we invited people to come forward to receive prayer from our ministry team at St Andrew's. I went to the door in order to say goodbye to all those who had come. After standing there only a few minutes, a man in his sixties came and asked if he could have a word with me. My normal practice is never to leave the entrance in order to focus on just one person but to make sure that I make contact with everyone. However, something in my spirit compelled me to say yes, so I sat down with this gentleman in the foyer of the church. He then related his story.

He told me that he was a pastor from another part of England who had travelled hours in order to be with us that night. He shared how he had been on sabbatical for four months and how he had been seeking the

Lord during that time for a touch of the Holy Spirit. He mentioned that his whole ministry had been a ministry of the word but not the Spirit, and that he had never experienced the reality of God's power in twenty-five years of church leadership. However, prior to going on sabbatical he had started teaching his church members that they needed to know the power of God as well as the scriptures. He also informed them that he was going to use his four months leave as a time for asking God to fill him with his Holy Spirit. A number of people left the church in protest, but the pastor persevered. He wanted his congregation to be charismatic as well as conservative. He exhorted them to use the four months of his absence in order to be filled with the Holy Spirit themselves.

As he looked at me, I could tell that there was genuine desperation in his heart. He told me that this was the last Sunday before returning to work and that he still hadn't experienced the fire of God. So I took him to the front and, together with George and Margaret, I began to pray for him. After a few moments I recalled the word that had been given in the prayer meeting before the service and I said, 'Tonight, brother, you are going to receive your certificate of spiritual adoption.' At that moment, he started swaying and repeating the words, 'Oh, that's lovely.' This continued for a few moments before he was overwhelmed by the Spirit. He lay on the ground for a few moments before Margaret touched his lips with her hand. Immediately he started speaking in tongues. The new language he used to praise his Father in heaven was extraordinarily beautiful.[8]

You see the point? It's not just that adoption enriches our image of God, it also enriches our experience of God. As the spirit of adoption is released without restraints in our hearts, so we begin to experience the glorious freedom of the children of God. We are impacted by amazing grace and, in response, we are set free to adore the Father with a language as simple as a child's! Though we may not experience precisely the same phenomena as this pastor, we will be free to know God as Father.

It enriches our service of God
This is perhaps the final, compelling motivation for exploring and experiencing our spiritual adoption. Most Christians desire to serve God in some capacity or another. But not every Christian who serves God does

so from the right foundation. Many serve as slaves rather than as sons and daughters.

One of the reasons for this lies in the childhood experiences of Christian believers. Some members of our churches had fathers who were either physically or emotionally absent at a key point in their lives. This means that they find the idea of God as a loving Father very difficult to understand. Their sense of rejection and abandonment by their earthly father leads to a sense of mistrust in their heavenly Father. They can never quite believe that God is a Father who loves them, accepts them and is always there for them. Thus, instead of basing their Christian service on the knowledge of God's favour and faithfulness, they become driven people, always trying to earn God's acceptance and attract his attention through good works.

Recently, I was speaking about spiritual adoption at a conference. A lady called Barbara came up to the platform after my talk and shared her story. She told us how her mother had died on Barbara's first birthday and how she had then been adopted by an elderly couple. When she was ten years old, she was informed about her past and told that she was an adopted child. She was also asked never to mention this again.

Later on in her life, Barbara became a committed Christian and later a minister's wife. However, her infant experience of rejection and her subsequent upbringing radically affected her ability to relate to God. From the moment that she was told about her adoption onwards, Barbara found that she was always under a burden to please her adoptive parents and couldn't bear the thought of letting them down in any way. This had a negative impact on her life as a minister's wife because she was always striving to be accepted by the people in her church and would constantly worry about the slightest sign of rejection (particularly in church business meetings).

Not long ago, however, Barbara went away for the weekend on a retreat designed to help people find wholeness through Christ. During a meeting, a woman who had never met her before came up to her and shared these words: 'You have been doubting that you are a child of God. I want to tell you—you are God's darling daughter!' That had a profound effect on Barbara and she has had a sense of her daughterhood in God's eyes ever since. No longer does she strive to earn the Father's approval and acceptance through performance. She now daily lives in the revelation that she is accepted and loved by Abba, Father.

Here is another story, this time from a woman in our church called Jane, who is currently serving the Lord as a Christian missionary in Pakistan. This also reflects how the Spirit of adoption enriches our service of God.

If we have received good teaching in our local church fellowship, we know a lot of things about God: that he is a loving Father; that we have become his children, never to be forsaken or abandoned. But our relationship with our earthly father and the various circumstances of our lives, mean that in our hearts—from where the core realities flow—we actually believe and act out in our lives a very different message about God.

My Christian life has been a journey to know God as he really is. I committed my life to Jesus Christ after hearing a talk entitled, 'Can God be known?' It connected with my deep-felt need for a personal relationship with a God who, knowing me completely, loved me and accepted me, and through the gift of his Son, invited me into an intimate, growing relationship.

The reality, however, for many years was very different. God was someone I had to keep on the right side of, who was intolerant of mistakes and before whom I needed to earn acceptance.

When I was seven years old, I had a serious operation. I was in hospital for several weeks and afterwards was sent to a convalescent home in a different part of the country for three months. Both experiences were very traumatic for me. My parents were only allowed to visit me once a fortnight for two hours. The sight of them disappearing behind the iron gates of the lift is a powerful memory. Through my internal lens the whole experience was characterized by unkindness, injustice, loneliness and a sense of abandonment. It left me with an inner determination never to put myself in a situation where I could experience that kind of pain again.

I never realized that its effects were still present in my life until January 1995. I had spent many weeks at the end of services just weeping. I didn't really understand what was happening except that I felt broken inside and that I was crying out to God from the depths of my heart. Looking back I believe God was softening my heart, melting the self-protective shell, so that he could bring further healing.

During a retreat at St Andrew's Church, Chorleywood, God moved powerfully in my life, especially during the times of worship. I got to the point where I didn't want any more and was ready to close down on God. But through the tears I recognized that life was nothing without him and that I wanted his will for my life. I found myself having to face the pain of that sense of abandonment that had taken root all those years ago and throw myself on God. It felt like jumping off a cliff not knowing if I would land safely, but finding the overwhelming love and faithfulness of God.

The healing that God gave has brought me into a place of greater intimacy with him. Living as a single woman in a Muslim country requires me to be secure in who I am and to have a source of deep affirmation. The Christian life is not essentially about having an emotional experience, but if I do not feel God's love daily, this is less than what my Father intends and has made provision for. Being with God is now my most secure place. In his presence I receive renewed strength and purpose to reach out to others who themselves need to know that they are not rejected or abandoned people but those who have a Father who puts infinite value on our lives and who has adopted us into his family.

This very moving testimony gives us a wonderful picture of how the loving spirit of adoption releases us from the wounds of the past and liberates us into serving the Father with hearts made whole. Knowing that she is adopted, accepted and affirmed by the Father has set Jane free to serve God in a very demanding mission field. Like all those who have experienced the grace of spiritual adoption, Jane serves the Lord out of gratitude rather than guilt. Instead of trying to earn God's acceptance through her ministry, she begins with the knowledge that she is an adopted daughter of the glorious Father. This is the basis of her identity, the source of her security, and the motivation for her ministry. Knowing and experiencing one's spiritual adoption is therefore of critical importance. It enriches our image of God, our experience of God, and our service of God. Indeed, in the case of the last of these, the adopted child of God is truly the one who discovers perfect freedom.

THE LOST COIN

In his recent book *The Theology of the Apostle Paul* (1998), Jimmy Dunn highlights the importance of the concept of adoption in Paul's theology. He sees significance in the similarities in Paul's language in the following two verses:

Because you are sons, God sent the Spirit of his Son into our hearts, the Spirit who calls out, 'Abba, Father.'
GALATIANS 4:6

For you did not receive a spirit that makes you a slave again to fear, but you received the Spirit of adoption. And by him we cry, 'Abba, Father.'
ROMANS 8:15

Why are the similarities between these two verses so revealing? Here is Dunn:

The fact that Paul makes such a similar reference in letters to two different churches (only one of which he knew personally) is a clear enough indication that the sense of sonship, both experienced in and expressed through the 'Abba' prayer, was common in most churches of the diaspora.[9]

Dunn is surely making a valid point here. That Paul could talk in such a similar way to two different churches proves the centrality of adoption in his theology and experience. However, having made this point, it is extraordinary that Dunn only mentions the concept of adoption on two pages in the whole of his book (which is 800 pages in length)! For Dunn to demonstrate how important a concept is and then only look at it twice seems strange to me.

Once again I am led to say that *the doctrine of adoption is the lost coin of*

Christian theology. It has been overshadowed and obscured by our focus on the doctrine of justification. Earlier I quoted Jim Packer's remark that the main reason for this has been the tendency of those after Luther to emphasize justification by faith to the neglect of adoption through the Spirit. In his classic book, *Knowing God*, Packer contrasts justification and adoption thus:

Justification is a forensic idea, conceived in terms of law, and viewing God as judge. In justification, God declares of penitent believers that they are not, and never will be, liable to the death that their sins deserve, because Jesus Christ, their substitute and sacrifice, tasted death in their place on the cross.

But contrast this, now, with adoption. Adoption is a family idea, conceived in terms of love, and viewing God as father. In adoption, God takes us into his family and fellowship, and establishes us as his children and heirs. Closeness, affection and generosity are at the heart of the relationship. To be right with God the judge is a great thing, but to be loved and cared for by God is a greater.[10]

Recently, Clark Pinnock has been restating Packer's argument. Pinnock has written the following:

Martin Luther's experience of salvation as justification has skewed the Christian understanding somewhat towards legal terms. Emphasis has been placed on the sinner's change of status, from guilty to not guilty, rather than on personal union with God. While Luther caught an aspect of the truth, a more relational model is required. Spirit is leading us to union—to transforming, personal, intimate relationship with the triune God.[11]

In actual fact, Pinnock is being too hard on Luther. While it is true that Luther's followers emphasized justification and neglected adoption, Packer rightly states that 'Luther's grasp of adoption was as strong and clear as his grasp of justification'.[12] It has been the post-Lutheran evangelicals, then, who have neglected the doctrine of adoption. Indeed, Packer shows that even the Puritans failed to highlight the truth of our adoption adequately. As I have already revealed, it is only in seasons of the Spirit (i.e. revivals) that the doctrine of adoption has been given its rightful place. In those contexts, the driving force for this has been the actual experience of adoption in the lives of believers.

A time to celebrate

The parable of the lost coin ends with a party. Jesus says that when the woman found the coin, she called her friends and neighbours together and said, 'Rejoice with me; I have found my lost coin.' This note of rejoicing is strong in Luke 15 as a whole. When the shepherd finds his lost sheep, he calls his friends and neighbours together in order to rejoice with him. When the lost son comes home, his father says, 'Let's have a feast and celebrate!' Whenever a single sinner comes to a place of repentance, Jesus says there is rejoicing in the presence of the angels of God.

Recently, a man in his early sixties called Allan started attending St Andrew's with his wife, Jenny. They came to our Alpha course and, as a result, committed their lives to Jesus Christ. One morning—shortly after the Alpha course—Allan came down for a cup of tea and a prayer. As he did so, the Holy Spirit led him to write a poem.

Before you read this poem, let me just say that Allan had never written a poem before this. He is not a sophisticated man of letters, by his own admission. Yet the Lord gave this wonderfully down-to-earth man a prophetic insight into the Father's heart, and he has given permission for me to share it with you. This is what the Holy Spirit led him to write:

I was lost in the wilderness but not alone,
When the voice of my Father said I must atone.
'Come walk with me and you will see
How I, your Father, can set you free.

Each step of the way I will be your guide,
I will never fail to be at your side.
When trouble comes and burdens you,
I will lighten the load as I always do.

So walk with me, my friend, my son,
Empty your heart of a past that's done.
Ask forgiveness, I will forgive.
Ask for a new life, I'll let you live.

Don't be afraid of the changes I make;
I will only make them for your sake.
But you must also do your part,
And keep me safely in your heart.

And remember this I say to you,
I shall watch over all that you do.
Go forward now, I've set you free—
Free to always be with me.'

From Orphans to Heirs is a *celebration* of the rediscovery of a lost coin. It is a call to celebrate the fact that the Father has adopted us as his sons and daughters. It is a summons to enjoy the highest blessing of the gospel. It is an invitation to make merry over the glorious truth that we do not need to live as slaves, striving to earn the Father's acceptance through good works. We already have that acceptance and we can know it through the power of the Holy Spirit.

My prayer is this: that you will take hold of this lost coin, brush the dust off it, and study it carefully. On one side of it you will find a picture of one far greater than any monarch—the High King of Heaven, your heavenly 'Abba'. As you study this portrait, I pray that the Holy Spirit will reveal something of the light of the Father's countenance as he smiles at you, his beloved, adopted child. I pray that you will see the words engraved around the edge of this coin: 'The Father himself loves you' (John 16:27).

On the other side of the coin you will see the cross, the means by which the Father's love was demonstrated. You will see the currency of heaven's mercy—not sterling, yen, roubles or dollars, but the blood of our Lord Jesus Christ.

A time to love

At the same time, my prayer is that the loving Spirit of adoption would not only cause you to fall in love with the Father. My prayer is that the same Spirit will also give us a greater compassion for the fatherless generation whose heart cry is audible everywhere today.

In Britain today, there are 50,000 children in care, 10,000 of them in residential homes. Local councils are spending 500 million pounds to keep them there rather than finding suitable parents who might adopt them. The reason for this is because adoption has become the last resort today. It is seen as a final option rather than something positive.

The British Agency for Adoption and Fostering has found that some local authorities are failing to make any adoptions at all. Whereas in the 1970s 21,000 children were being adopted each year, today the number is just 2,000. While the number of children being committed to care is increasing by approximately five per cent each year, the number of children being adopted is dramatically decreasing. In many local authorities, children are being denied the opportunity of being brought up in a loving family atmosphere because of the colour of their (or their parents') skin. Not only is this desperately unfair for the many unadopted children in our nation. It is also producing a fatherless generation bent on crime. Indeed, children who spend long periods in care are fifty times more likely to end up in prison as those who don't. They make up 26 per cent of the adult prison population.

As you read this book, my hope is that we will not only learn to love the Lord our God with a fresh passion. My hope is that we will also receive an increase in compassion for those who don't know this love. There are many literal orphans who need to know that God is a father to the fatherless. There are even more spiritual orphans who need to know this. May the Lord not only restore the Great Commandment to his church. May he also restore the Great Commission.

CHAPTER 2

Adopting Grace

When Philip and Joy Stibbe adopted me in 1960, they followed a recognized legal procedure involving the Social Services and the courts of England. When the apostle Paul wrote about our spiritual adoption in the New Testament, he was thinking of a recognized legal procedure in the world of the first century. It is now known that this procedure was not Jewish because there was no rite of adoption in the Judaism of Jesus' day. Indeed, there is no teaching on adoption in the Old Testament. So where do we need to look in order to find the background for this vital New Testament concept?

It is now commonly agreed that the Roman rite of adoption lies behind Paul's thinking.[13] So how did the Romans adopt children? In what follows I will paint a picture of one common adoption scenario in the Roman world of Jesus' day.[14]

Imagine the scene. We are in ancient Rome, around about the year 50BC. You are a Roman citizen with a beautiful wife called Maximilia (forgive the male perspective here). You have been married about five years and have been trying to have children. Pretty soon it has become clear that one of you is infertile and that your family name (the *pater familias*), so precious in Roman culture, is not going to be perpetuated unless you have a son.

Together you make the decision to adopt. So you look first of all to your own household, to the slaves who serve you. There you find a slave called Marcus who has a wife and four children, three of them boys. You go to Marcus and you ask whether he would be prepared to sell one of his boys for adoption. After long consideration, Marcus says yes.

Why do Marcus and his wife agree to this? First and foremost because it will mean that their son becomes a free man. The precarious and oppressive life of slavery is over. Secondly, because it means that their son will inherit the *pater familias* of their master and, in the process, become *sui heredes*. He will become the master's very own heir, and will inherit the master's entire estate. Thirdly, because it means that all the adopted son's previous debts will be cancelled on joining his new family. What may seem a heartless act to us—the sale of a son—is therefore an act of kindness.

So the whole process of adoption begins. You go with Marcus and the boy to the local Roman magistrate. Proceedings known as *Adoptio Sensu Strictu* begin with all of you standing before the magistrate. Three times the natural father sells the boy to the new father and on each occasion the magistrate watches as the boy is passed from one to the other.

After the third transaction, the magistrate makes the declaration: 'This boy is now adopted as your son.' The money passes hands from the adopting father to the natural father, and the boy is now legally *sui heredes*, the new father's son and heir. He has been taken out from under the *patria potestas* of Marcus the slave, and placed under a new *patria potestas* (meaning 'fatherly authority'). The boy now has the status of a free person. All previous debts are cancelled. The boy has a new family and a new future.

SPIRITUAL ADOPTION

When we think of the Roman rite of adoption from our contemporary perspective, it is all too easy to regard Marcus as a callous man and the whole ritual as somewhat unloving. In reality, however, seen within its own cultural context, the whole business is an act of emancipation. A boy with no privileges or opportunities has been delivered from an often dangerous life of servitude and given the full rights of a wealthy son.

The apostle Paul was not only a Jewish rabbi and a Christian apostle, he was also a Roman citizen. When the Holy Spirit began to reveal to him the great mystery of God's love in Christ, one of the images that came to his mind was the Roman one of 'adoption'. On five occasions in his letters, Paul therefore employed the picture of *Adoptio Sensu Strictu* in order to portray the wonderful truth that we have been delivered from slavery into sonship:

But when the time had fully come, God sent his Son, born of a woman, born under law, to redeem those under law, the we might receive adoption.
GALATIANS 4:4–5

In love God predestined us to be adopted as his sons through Jesus Christ, in accordance with his pleasure and will.
EPHESIANS 1:5

For you did not receive a spirit that makes you a slave again to fear, but you received the Spirit of adoption. And by him we cry, 'Abba, Father'.
ROMANS 8:15

We ourselves, who have the firstfruits of the Spirit, groan inwardly as we wait eagerly for our adoption, the redemption of our bodies.
ROMANS 8:23

Theirs [i.e. Israel's] is the adoption as sons; theirs the divine glory, the covenants, the receiving of the law, the temple worship and the promises.
ROMANS 9:4

In each of these statements, Paul uses the same word when he speaks of adoption. Paul wrote in a popular form of Greek known as 'koine Greek'. Even though the concept of adoption is a Roman one, he therefore explored it using a Greek word, *huiothesia*. Behind this lies the picture of the Roman magistrate making the pronouncement, 'You are an adopted son!' The person adopted was often the son of a slave in Paul's day. His adoption led to what is called his 'manumission' or liberation.

Now marvel with me at the spiritual application of this picture. The story of what is known as our 'salvation history' can be summed up as a journey from slavery to sonship, involving a process of spiritual adoption. Before you and I became believers, we were living as orphans and slaves. We did not know God as our Father. We were under the *patria potestas* of Satan, the father of lies. We were weighed down by the heavy debt of sin and consequently 'separate from Christ, excluded from citizenship in Israel and foreigners to the covenants of the promise, without hope and without God in the world' (Ephesians 2:12).

However, at the perfect time the Father sent his one and only Son into the world so that we would be delivered from slavery. Jesus, who was in very nature God, emptied himself and took the nature of a slave and became obedient to death, even death on a cross (Philippians 2:6–8). He died a slave's death on a rubbish tip outside Jerusalem in order that we might be set free from our slavery to sin. Put another way, *the Son became a slave so that we, who were slaves, might become sons*. We will be exploring this glorious truth in greater detail in Chapter 4.

In the diagram below you will see in pictorial form something of the human condition before Jesus died for our sins at Calvary. Before Jesus died on the cross, we are on the left hand side, trying desperately to get out of slavery through good works and religious lives:

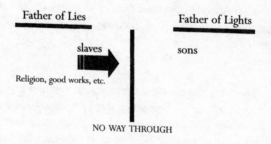

When Jesus died on the cross, all that was needed to pay for our adoption was provided not through gold or silver but through the precious blood that he shed at Calvary (1 Peter 1:18–19). If we want to become God's sons and daughters, we must therefore believe that Jesus paid the adoption price on the cross, that he died to set us free from sin, and accept him as our Saviour and Lord. When we make that decision, we break through the sin barrier with saving faith as opposed to good works. The cross is therefore the bridge over which we must travel if we want to be delivered from slavery into sonship.

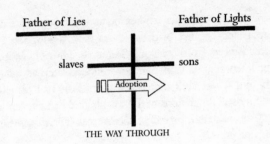

THE WAY THROUGH

This shows how vital the cross is to our adoption. As a result of the Calvary love of God, we are now faced with a choice: Do we want to be set free or not? Do we want to come out from under the *patria postestas* of Satan and be placed under the *patria potestas* of our heavenly Abba? Do we want to hear the words of the Judge of All declaring us 'adopted as sons and daughters'? If we do, then the journey from slavery to sonship can be made today. The key to making the journey is to repent of our sins and believe in Jesus. Here are the steps we need to take in order to be adopted by our heavenly Abba:

Admit that we are sinners—more than that, that we're slaves to sin, and that we are powerless to escape from this slavery by our own merits.

Believe that Jesus is God's Son and that he died to pay the debt of sin; confess that the Son became a slave that we who are slaves might become sons.

Commit ourselves to following Jesus for the rest of our lives, to living life as a son and resisting all forms of slavery, till the day we die.

THE PRINCE OF EGYPT

Adoption is therefore a picture taken from the Roman world. Having said that, Paul was not only a Roman citizen and a Christian apostle, he was also a Jewish rabbi. Although there is no rite of adoption mentioned in the Hebrew Bible, Paul's Jewish temperament would have found this concept appealing because of the story of Israel's adoption by God. In other words, Paul loved to speak of God as an adopting Father not only because he knew that all Christian believers had been adopted, but also because he knew very well that Israel as a whole had experienced this privilege. Out of all the nations of the world, God had chosen one nation, Israel, to be his adopted, precious, special son. The theologians call this God's 'electing grace'.

Let's explore this truth in the form of a fictional story:

When God was looking for a people to call his own, he went to all the peoples of the world and he asked them what they would do if he became their God and they became his people.

He asked the Greeks, 'If I became your God and you became my people, what would you do for me?' And the Greeks said, 'Master of the Universe, if you become our God and we become your people, we will create for you the most beautiful works of art and the most profound systems of philosophy the world has ever known. All the people will come and worship you because of your beauty and your wisdom.' And God said, 'Thank you', and he went on.

And God went to the Romans and he asked, 'If I became your God and you became my people, what would you do for me?' The Romans said, 'Almighty God, if you become our God and we become your people, we will set your standard at the head of our armies and we will put your banner before the caravans and the fleets of our commercial empire. All people will come and bow down before you because of your power and your might.' And God said, 'Thank you', and he went on.

And God went to all the peoples of the world and got their offers. Finally he came to a scrawny bunch of nomads in the desert called Hebrews. Now these nomads were shrewd traders and God said to them, 'If I became your God and you became my people, what will you do for me?' And the people said, 'Lord God, we cannot offer you great works of art or systems of philosophy. It is not within our capability. Nor can we offer you great power or wealth. You can see our poor herds and tents. But if you become our God and we become your people, we will tell the stories of your deeds to our children and they to their children and they to their children to all generations.'

And God said, 'It's a deal!'

'It's a deal!' God chose Israel out of all the nations of the world to be his adopted son. He chose one of the most insignificant groups of people and, in the process, made them the most significant nation in history. He took a very ordinary community of people and conferred on them the most extraordinary purpose. Why? Because our God is an adopting Father. Out of sheer grace he chooses to embrace people in the enfolding circle of his love. Thus, fifteen hundred years before the birth of Jesus, God took hold of a man called Abram and made this promise to him (Genesis 12:1–3):

> *I will make you into a great nation*
>   *and I will bless you;*
> *I will make your name great,*
>   *and you will be a blessing.*
> *I will bless those who bless you,*
>   *and whoever curses you I will curse;*
> *and all peoples on earth*
>   *will be blessed through you.*

All those centuries ago, God called and chose two people—Abraham and Sarah—to be the parents of a new nation. Subsequently, they had a son, Isaac, and he in turn had a son called Jacob. Jacob's youngest son Joseph was sold into slavery and was taken from Canaan to Egypt.

It was in Egypt over the next 430 years that God made the descendants of Abraham into a great nation (Genesis 46:3). After Joseph died, the Israelites multiplied so much that the land of Egypt was filled with them (Exodus 1:7). A new Pharaoh who had not known Joseph came to power and became alarmed at the number of Israelites in his kingdom. The Egyptians therefore turned them into slaves and worked them ruthlessly. They made their lives bitter with hard labour (Exodus 1:11–14).

However, the Lord raised up a man called Moses, born of Levite parents, but abandoned as a baby. Having been placed in a papyrus basket and left on the waters of the Nile, Moses was discovered by Pharaoh's daughter, who adopted him into her family. The narrator of the book of Exodus tells us, 'he became her son' (Exodus 2:10). When Moses grew up, he pleaded with Pharaoh to let the Israelites leave Egypt. God sent ten plagues upon the Egyptians before the Israelites were permitted to leave. When permission was eventually granted, the exodus occurred and the Israelites began their journey back to Canaan, the Promised Land.

The nation of Israel was really formed at the exodus. It was only when the Israelites came out from under the oppression of the Egyptians that they became a separate people. It is only when they were given the Commandments at Mount Sinai that they received the divine instructions that would enable them to develop their own distinctive identity as a nation. From this point onwards, the people of Israel enjoyed a special status as God's adopted son. The beautiful words of Deuteronomy 7:7–8 say it all:

The Lord did not set his affection on you and choose you because you were more numerous than other peoples, for you were the fewest of all peoples. But it was because the Lord loved you and kept the oath he swore to your forefathers that he brought you out with a mighty hand and redeemed you from the land of slavery, from the power of Pharaoh king of Egypt.

FROM SLAVERY TO SONSHIP

In this great act of love, the Father adopted the people of Israel into a filial relationship with himself. Throughout the Old Testament, there are a number of references to the adoptive sonship that God confers upon Israel. Perhaps the most moving of all these references is in Hosea 11:1ff., where God reminds the prophet of his love for Israel:

When Israel was a child, I loved him,
and out of Egypt I called my son...
I led them with cords of human kindness,

> *with ties of love;*
> *I lifted the yoke from their neck*
> *and bent down to feed them.*

In Egypt, the Israelites were driven by whips. In the exodus, they were drawn by cords of love. When they left Egypt, the Father's plan and promise of adoption was actualized in their experience.[15] At the exodus, God used an adopted child (Moses) to lead his people into the reality of their promised adoption. Indeed, the Lord instructed Moses to say to Pharaoh, 'This is what the Lord says: Israel is my firstborn son, and I told you, "Let my son go, so that he may worship me"' (Exodus 4:22–23).

The exodus from Egypt was therefore a journey from slavery to sonship. At the start of this chapter, I showed how Paul's concept of 'adoption' is taken from the context of the Roman law courts. In the Roman rite of adoption, the child being adopted would be sold three times by the natural parent. More often than not, the child up for adoption would be a slave. After the third time the child had been sold, the transaction would be complete, and he would come out from under his own father's authority and be placed under his new, adoptive father's authority. From that moment on, the son would be regarded in the same light as a son who had been naturally born to his adoptive parents. He would be a rightful inheritor of his new parent's estate.

Paul says of the people of Israel, 'Theirs is the adoption [*huiothesia*] as sons' (Romans 9:4). When God called Israel out of Egypt, a transaction took place between God and Pharaoh. Ten times God told Pharaoh to let his people go. Nine times Pharaoh said no. After the tenth time, when Egypt's own first-born sons were killed, Pharaoh finally relented and the exchange was complete. God redeemed Israel from slavery. In the process, the Israelites came out from under the authority of Pharaoh and came under God's authority. God's authority over Israel was established at Sinai when the Torah was given to Moses. Here God revealed his fatherly love by giving Israel instructions on how to live a holy life. God says in Deuteronomy 8:5: 'Know then in your heart that as a man disciplines his son, so the Lord your God disciplines you.'

From this moment on, Israel became the heir of what the Father had promised to Abraham. Through adoption, Israel became the privileged recipient of the Father's estate:

The Lord your God is bringing you into a good land—a land with streams and pools of water, with springs flowing in the valleys and hills; a land with wheat and barley, vines and fig trees, pomegranates, olive oil and honey; a land where bread will not be scarce and you will lack nothing; a land where the rocks are iron and you can dig copper out of the hills.

DEUTERONOMY 8:7–9

FROM SONSHIP TO SLAVERY

Having received such a privilege, you would think that Israel would have lived in a state of constant appreciation. Unfortunately, that is not the case. On the one hand, it is true that God chose the people of Israel and loved them as a father. On the other hand, Israel did not always choose to live in obedience to God and frequently rebelled against him. The beautiful passage from Hosea 11 that I have already quoted portrays this awful tragedy in words that highlight the Father's grief:

When Israel was a child, I loved him,
*   and out of Egypt I called my son.*
But the more I called Israel,
*   the further they went from me.*
They sacrificed to the Baals
*   and they burned incense to images.*

Though God had adopted Israel as his son, Israel rejected him and rebelled. Instead of worshipping their heavenly Father, the Israelites turned to foreign idols. In the process they pierced the Father's heart with the wound of undeserved rejection.

What was the consequence of Israel's rebellion? The principal result was that Israel experienced the exact reverse of the exodus. At the exodus, Israel was led out of slavery into sonship. When Israel rebelled against the

Father, the opposite occurred; Israel was led out of the experience of sonship into the experience of slavery. When Israel was conquered by the Babylonians in 597BC, the survivors were led from the land that the Lord had given them into exile in Babylon. There they returned to the experience of Egypt. They lived in a foreign land under the authority of a pagan ruler. They were far from home and far from free. Thus, *at the exodus, Israel was led from the experience of slavery into the experience of sonship. At the exile, Israel was led from the experience of sonship into the experience of slavery.*

Though the Father never stopped loving Israel as his adopted son, the exiled people of Israel lost the privileges of sonship in their subjective experience. However, a faithful remnant wept by the rivers of Babylon and implored God to remember his commitment to Israel as his son:

You, O Lord, are our Father,
our Redeemer from of old is your name.
ISAIAH 63:16

This remnant of repentant people cried out to God to turn from anger and remember mercy:

Yet, O Lord, you are our Father.
We are the clay, you are the potter;
we are all the work of your hand.
Do not be angry beyond measure, O Lord;
do not remember our sins for ever.
Oh, look upon us we pray,
for we are all your people.
ISAIAH 64:8–9

The Father heard these prayers and in 538BC, Zerubbabel was allowed to return to the land of Israel with 50,000 exiles. The second temple was completed in 516BC and, for a while, Israel worshipped the Lord once again.

However, in the centuries that followed, the same pattern of behaviour was repeated. Once again Israel rebelled. Once again Israel was led from the experience of sonship to the experience of slavery. By the time Jesus was born, the people of Israel were experiencing the oppressive reality of Roman occupation. They were living once again as slaves rather than as sons. Consequently, the Abrahamic promise was not being fulfilled. Israel was not seizing its destiny and bringing the nations into the orbit of the Father's blessing. Therefore, God sent Jesus, his one and only Son, to achieve what Israel had not achieved. Thus, Jesus embodies so much of Israel's history in the story of his own life. Notice the parallels between Israel's history and Jesus':

- Both are called the son of God (though Jesus was the natural Son of God, Israel was God's son by adoption).
- Both births were miraculous (Jesus' by Mary, Israel's by Sarah).
- Both went into Egypt and were subsequently called out of Egypt.
- Both were despised and rejected.
- Both were put to death by the Romans.

Truly, Jesus is a microcosm of Israel.

Now, through Jesus, the promise made to Abraham can at last be fulfilled. After Jesus' death on the cross, after his resurrection and ascension, he pours out the Holy Spirit on the Day of Pentecost, and he pours it out on all flesh. Within a short time Gentiles are experiencing salvation. Members of the non-Jewish nations are being brought into the Father's arms of love through the followers of Jesus. The Abrahamic promise is now becoming a reality through Jesus and his twelve disciples—the representatives of True Israel. Those who believe in Jesus are now no longer slaves but the adopted sons and daughters of God (Galatians 3:26). As Paul puts it:

If you belong to Christ, then you are Abraham's seed, and heirs according to the promise.
GALATIANS 3:29

More than that,

You are no longer a slave, but a son; and since you are a son, God has made you also an heir.
GALATIANS 4:7

A FAMILY WITH JEWISH ROOTS

When Paul speaks about spiritual adoption he is therefore thinking as a Roman, a Jew and a Christian, and speaking in Greek! As a Roman Christian, he was thinking of the process of *Adoptio Sensu Strictu* through which believers in Jesus are brought out of slavery into sonship. Indeed the parallels between what would have happened to a Roman slave and what has happened to us are striking:

ROMAN ADOPTION	OUR ADOPTION
• A father chooses to adopt a son.	• Abba decides to adopt us.
• The adopted son is a slave.	• We are slaves spiritually.
• The adopting father pays for his new son.	• Our adoption is paid through the blood of Christ.
• The adopted son is set free from slavery.	• At our adoption, we are given glorious freedom.
• The adopted son comes out from under his former father's authority.	• The new believer is delivered from Satan's dominion.
• The magistrate declares the boy to be adopted as a son.	• Our Father declares, 'You are my beloved son/daughter.'
• He is placed under the *patria potestas* of his new father.	• We come under God the Father's authority.
• He has a new family.	• We join the family of God.
• He becomes *sui heredes*.	• We become co-heirs with Christ.
• All previous debts are cancelled.	• The debt of sin is paid for in full; we start life afresh.
• The boy learns to call his new father 'Pater'.	• We call out 'Abba!' to God.

Having said that, Paul not only thinks as a Roman, he thinks as a Jew. Thus, for him, adoption is a concept that can be applied to Israel's history as well (Deuteronomy 1:31). Even Moses—the one who led the people of Israel out of Egypt—embodies the truth of Israel's adoption. He himself had been adopted by Pharaoh's daughter, thereby making a journey from slavery to sonship. Joseph before him had, in a less obvious way, embodied the same story.[16]

Thus, Paul can make a comparison in his own mind between the Roman rite of adoption and what had happened to Israel:

ROMAN ADOPTION	ISRAEL'S ADOPTION
• A father decides to adopt a son.	• Yahweh decides to adopt Israel.
• The adopted son is a slave.	• Before entering into sonship, Israel is enslaved in Egypt.
• The adopted son is set free.	• At the exodus, Israel is freed.
• The adopted son comes out from under his previous father's authority.	• Israel comes out from under the *patria potestas* of Pharoah.
• The magistrate declares the boy to be an adopted son.	• Yahweh declares that Israel is his firstborn son.
• He is placed under the *patria potestas* of his new father.	• At Sinai, Israel comes under Yahweh's authority.
• He becomes *sui heredes*, the new father's heir.	• Israel is fully established as the heir of the Abrahamic promise.

In the light of all this, it is extremely important that Gentile (that is, non-Jewish) Christians recognize their rich heritage. When we are born again and adopted as God's sons and daughters, we join the family of Israel. This is the main theme of Romans 9—11. There Paul stresses that Israel was adopted first and that Gentile believers are grafted in to the olive tree of Israel. This is what Paul says of Israel's privileges in Romans 9:4–5:

Theirs is the adoption as sons; theirs the divine glory, the covenants, the receiving of the law, the temple worship and the promises. Theirs are the patriarchs, and from them is traced the human ancestry of Christ, who is God over all, for ever praised! Amen.

The fact that Paul can put *huiothesia* or adoption first in the list of Israel's privileges shows that it has pride of place in Paul's thought.

When I was adopted, I entered a family with a rich history on my father's side. My father's family has Jewish roots and originated in the Netherlands ('Stibbe' is a Dutch name). Indeed, my mother has traced the Stibbes back to the seventeenth century, and there are a number of rabbis in our family tree. Recently I visited Yad Vashem, the Holocaust Memorial outside Jerusalem. From the records there I discovered that 124 Dutch Stibbes died in various death camps in Europe during the Holocaust. Many of these met terrible deaths in Auschwitz. Children as young as six were slaughtered. The family into which I have been adopted is truly one with a very rich, yet tragic, past.

It is so important for Christians—particularly Gentile Christians—to appreciate that they have been adopted not just into a personal relationship with the Father, but also into a spiritual family with Jewish roots. In other words, it is vital that we do not allow ourselves to develop a purely individualistic understanding of spiritual adoption. To be sure, every individual Christian has been adopted into God's family through the death of Jesus Christ. Every believer has the spirit of adoption at work in his or her life and is thereby enabled to enjoy an intimate relationship with God. But this is not where adoption begins and ends. We need to understand that the blessing of adoption is not just personal in application but has bigger implications than this. When we are adopted as the children of God, we do not stand alone in that blessing. We join a family that goes back to Abraham. The name of that family is Israel.

THE ADOPTING FATHER

What this shows is that right from the very beginning, God has been revealing his 'electing' or, better still, his 'adopting grace'. God has been revealing himself as the Abba who adopts children into the everlasting embrace of the Godhead. This is the image of God which we so desperately need to have revealed to us today. As we allow the Holy Spirit to testify to our spirits that we are children of God, and as we form our understanding of God from the fatherly qualities described in scripture, then we will be released from slavery into sonship. We will be truly liberated to worship the Father in spirit and in truth.

In the final analysis, the cry of the Father is this: 'Let my people go that they may worship me.' God's great desire is for his people to be set free from all forms of slavery so that they may enjoy intimacy with him in worship. For too long the evil one has been holding God's people captive, bewitching them with the lie that they have to earn God's acceptance through punctilious observance of rules and regulations. This has led to a cold formalistic religion in which God has been kept very much at arm's length. Today, however, there is a liberating move of the Holy Spirit in the churches. Paul wrote that where the Spirit of the Lord is, there is freedom. How true that is! There is a chain-breaking work of God going on in which his children are being set free to worship him as Abba, Father. This is particularly true amongst young people (Generation X). This 'fatherless' generation is rediscovering the wonderful truth that God is a Father who calls, loves and keeps his children (Jude, verse 1). In the process, a whole generation of radical worshippers is being raised up (Psalm 24:3–6).

One Bible passage that has spoken to many people in recent years is Zephaniah 3:17. In its original context, this verse refers to the restoration of the city of Jerusalem in the time of Ezra and Nehemiah. However, many believers have felt the immediate significance of this particular verse in their personal relationship with Abba, Father. Many have taken the prophet's words to heart and seen them as a window on to the Father heart of God:

The Lord will take great delight in you,
  he will quiet you with his love,
  he will rejoice over you with singing.

Three things are said here about the way the Father views those who are adopted as his sons and daughters. First of all, the Father takes great delight in us. It does not say that he takes great delight in what we do. It says that he takes great delight in who we are. If we are 'in Christ', then he has great pleasure in us. The words he spoke to Jesus at his baptism, he says to us: 'You are my son/daughter, whom I love; with you I am well pleased.'

Secondly, it says that he will quiet us with his love. In other words, the Father woos us into a place of security and serenity by revealing the depth of his love for us. We do not have to strive and shout to earn his love. It is simply there to be revealed through the gentle whispers of his gracious Spirit.

Thirdly—and most wonderfully of all—it says that the Father rejoices over us with singing. What a thought that is! Just as an earthly father sometimes serenades his child with a bedtime lullaby, so our heavenly Father sings over us. More than that, he sings over us a song of rejoicing!

It is this final thought that has been carried on the wings of the Spirit into the hearts of many today. The idea that the Father celebrates over us and sings a special song of joy about us is almost too good to be true. One of my great desires in life is to reach a point of such intimacy with the Father that I catch a few bars of the heavenly song that he sings over me personally. To use the words of Sam Storms, I want to hear 'the heavenly aria of God's unfathomable love'[17] for me. I want you to hear your song too. I want the lost to come to the Father's house and to hear the joyful refrains of the singing God as well.

What an amazing revelation this is! God is a Father who adopts us with joy, and who expresses that joy in song over each one of us. In the next chapter, we will celebrate in greater depth this glorious Father. Before that, just meditate for a few minutes on the adopting grace of God. Learn to rejoice in the fact that you are chosen. Be like the two adopted children of a member of my church. Their mother heard me preach on the adopting grace of God recently and she wrote the following in a letter:

I recall when our two children were young we frequently explained to them that we had adopted them (from a few weeks old in each case). I was reminded how sometimes they would say, 'I was chosen' in a proud voice. So it is wonderful to know that we too have been chosen!

CHAPTER 3

The Glorious Father

Forty years ago, a couple called Philip and Joy Stibbe had a beautiful baby boy whom they named Giles. Though the birth was extremely difficult, they were delighted with their first child and for a while all three were very happy. However, before Giles' birth, Philip and Joy had been advised by a specialist that they should not have any more children after their first child. Joy had been a nurse at Great Ormond Street Hospital and had been exposed to many X-rays as part of her job, particularly during the Second World War when she spent a lot of her time tending the wounded there. There was therefore a very real danger that any further children might be affected adversely.

Naturally this was a source of sadness to Philip and Joy, but instead of grieving they made plans to adopt a child. After interviews and a good deal of paperwork, they found themselves several years later in an orphanage in Hackney. There they were invited to look at two twin babies. Though they had wanted only one more child, they realized that it was wrong to part these twins. They also began, even then and there, to feel affection for them both, and so—after the necessary legal formalities—they were brought home to live with Philip, Joy and Giles. Speaking as one of those twins, I have never regretted that homecoming for one moment.

THE FATHER'S PLAN

I begin with that story because I have always found it a vivid illustration of what the Father has done for each one of us. In Ephesians 1:3–8, Paul writes these magnificent words of praise:

Praise be to the God and Father of our Lord Jesus Christ, who has blessed us in the heavenly realms with every spiritual blessing in Christ. For he chose us in him before the creation of the world to be holy and blameless in his sight. In love he predestined us to be adopted as his sons through

Jesus Christ, in accordance with his pleasure and will—to the praise of his glorious grace, which he has freely given us in the One he loves. In him we have redemption through his blood, the forgiveness of his sins, in accordance with the riches of God's grace that he lavished on us with all wisdom and understanding.

The statement that has always caught my eye is in verse 5: 'In love he [the Father] predestined us to be adopted [*huiothesia*] as his sons through Jesus Christ, in accordance with his pleasure and will'. Before the world was made, before the first human being was formed, the Father decided that he was going to choose us to be part of his family. He made up his mind in advance to adopt us, and he planned that this process of adoption would be undertaken through the ministry of his one and only Son, Jesus Christ.

What finer insight could we have into the Father's plan for humanity? Just as Philip, Joy and Giles made up their minds in advance to adopt Claire and myself, so the Father decided in advance to adopt us into their family. If you are someone who has been born again, then you are a member of that eternal family. God is your Father. Jesus Christ is the brother who introduced you to the Father. The Holy Spirit is the one who enables you to relate to the Father as a son or a daughter. This is the greatest privilege in the universe—to receive the blessing of adoption that the Father has lavished upon us.

Our adoption as sons and daughters is one of the best of the Father's blessings! It is a great gift of the Trinity. Paul makes it clear that the whole of the Godhead was committed to the task of adopting us. In his great exclamation of praise just quoted, Paul speaks of the Father who has blessed us, in Christ the Son, with the blessings of the Holy Spirit. All three persons of the Godhead are therefore involved in our adoption as sons and daughters. The Triune God gave everything of himself for our adoption. In this chapter we will focus on the Father's role.

THE FATHER'S PASSION

In 1937 a man called John Griffiths managed to get a job tending one of the railroad bridges that crossed the Mississippi river.[18] Every day he would control the gears of the bridge to allow barges and ships through.

One day John decided to allow his eight-year-old son, Greg, to help him. He and his boy packed their lunches with great excitement and high hopes for the future and went to work. The morning went quickly and at noon they headed off for lunch, down a narrow catwalk on to an observation platform about 50 feet above the great river. John told Greg stories about the ships as they passed by.

Suddenly, they were jolted back to reality by the shrill sound of an engine's whistle. Looking at his watch, John realized to his horror that it was 1.07pm, that the Memphis Express was due any time and that the bridge was still raised.

He calmly told Greg to stay put and then ran back to the controls. Once there he looked beneath the bridge to make sure there was nothing below. As his eyes moved downwards he saw something so terrible that he froze. For there, lying on the gears, was his beloved son. Greg had tried to follow his dad but had fallen off the catwalk.

Immediately, John saw the horrifying choice before him: either to lower the bridge and kill his son, or to keep the bridge raised and kill everyone on board the train. As four hundred people moved closer to the bridge, John realized what he had to do. Burying his face under his arm, he plunged down the lever. The cries of his son were instantly drowned out by the noise of the bridge grinding slowly into position.

John wiped the tears from his eyes as the train passed by. A conductor was collecting tickets in his usual way. A businessman was casually reading a newspaper. Ladies were drinking afternoon tea. Children were playing. Most of the passengers were engaged in idle chatter. No one saw. No one heard the cries of a heartbroken father:

'Can't you see? Don't you care? I've sacrificed my son for you. What's the matter with you?'

This story gives us an insight into the Father's passion. To be sure, we know that Jesus Christ loved us to death on the cross. Every time we take Holy Communion we remember the depth of suffering love shown by the Son of God. But what about the suffering love of the Father?[19] Have we ever really paused to reflect on how he felt as he saw his beloved Son dying on the cross for you and for me? Have we ever stopped to imagine the grief he feels as the world goes merrily on, ignoring the sacrifice he made?

The truth is that the Father loves us with a selfless passion. The word 'passion' comes from a Latin word meaning 'suffering'. The Father's love for us is a love that costs, that hurts, that suffers. We need to remember that our adoption is free, but it is not cheap. It cost the Father dear to send his one and only Son, knowing we would reject, torture and kill him. As Stuart Townend, the songwriter, has recently put it:

> How deep the Father's love for us,
> How vast beyond all measure,
> That he should give His only Son
> To make a wretch His treasure.
> How great the pain of searing loss,
> The Father turns His face away,
> As wounds which mar the Chosen One
> Bring many sons to glory.[20]

THE FATHER'S PREDESTINATION

Having said all that, some may well be provoked to ask, 'What kind of love is this that chooses some but not all for adoption?' At this point we enter the issue of the Father's predestination. Paul, without embarrassment, says, 'The Father *predestined* us for adoption'. What, then, of those who have not been chosen? What about those millions who, in the course of human history, have not been adopted and have remained, as a result, spiritual orphans?

Here the analogy with my own experience breaks down. When Philip Stibbe came to the orphanage in Hackney, he and Joy chose to adopt just two children. With great sadness, they had to leave the rest behind, knowing that at least some of them might never have happy homes to go to. They had no plan for those who remained orphans.

With our heavenly Father, the situation is altogether different. Yes, the Father chose to adopt some people out of all the nations of the world. In the first instance, he chose to adopt one, insignificant nation called Israel. The rest were not chosen. In the second instance, when Israel rejected

God, he chose to send his only Son so that, through his saving death, people might be adopted from the Jewish and Gentile nations. In both cases, some were chosen, while many were not.

However, the Father has always had a plan for those whom he did not choose. Unlike my own father, our Father in heaven took steps to provide a home for all remaining orphans. His plan was as follows. He purposed to adopt some, and through them, to invite the rest. In other words, God chose a few but invited many. As Jesus put it in the Parable of the Wedding Banquet, 'many are invited but few are chosen' (Matthew 22:14). His plan was that the mankind should be given the invitation to come home into his house *through the minority that had already experienced his sovereign 'adopting grace'*. This means that his desire has always been that the many should be attracted into his family through the witness of those already adopted.

In the first instance, Israel's destiny was to be the chosen nation through which all peoples on earth would be blessed (Genesis 11:3). Through the one Jewish nation—Yahweh's adopted son—all the Gentile nations of the earth were to be invited into the Father's house. As Yahweh says in Isaiah 56:6–8:

> *And foreigners who bind themselves to the Lord*
> *   to serve him,*
> *to love the name of the Lord,*
> *   and to worship him,*
> *all who keep the Sabbath without desecrating it,*
> *   and who hold fast to my covenant—*
> *these I will bring to my holy mountain*
> *   and give them joy in my house of prayer.*
> *Their burnt offerings and sacrifices*
> *   will be accepted on my altar;*
> *for my house will be called*
> *   a house of prayer for all nations.*

Here we see God as the Father who wants to gather all the spiritual orphans in this world into his house. We see his sovereign purpose: to have his adopted son, Israel, invite everyone—even the *goyim*, foreigners or Gentiles—into the secure arms of his covenant love. Put in pictorial form, the Father's purpose for Israel looked like Figure 1 below.

Tragically, Israel did not seize its destiny to be the nation through whom the Gentiles could come home to the Father. This is the real reason why Jesus' heart burnt with anger when he entered the temple precincts in the last week of his life. Instead of finding the Court of the Gentiles occupied by people praying for the nations and welcoming non-Jews, he found it full of money-changers and commercial stalls. By this stage Jesus had already chosen a group of disciples, so after his death and resurrection he gave them the mission originally given to Israel. Now, out of these chosen people, all nations were to be told the good news (Matthew 28:18–20).

On top of that, through the ministry of Paul, apostle to the Gentiles, the promise given to Abraham can now at last be realized. Through the faithful remnant of Israel, all the peoples of the earth can be blessed! Through the Jewish followers of Jesus, the world can be invited (Figure 2).

Far from seeing the Father's predestination as a negative thing, we should therefore see it in a positive light. This is the way the Father has always wanted to bless all the peoples of the earth—through chosen, adopted people. It may be true that few are chosen, but it is also true that everyone on the face of the earth who hears the Good News is invited to the Father's house. Everyone is invited to come home to the Father.

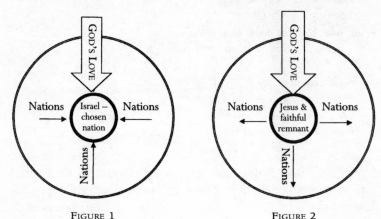

FIGURE 1   FIGURE 2

THE FATHER'S PLEASURE

While the Father grieves over every child that remains a spiritual orphan, he also delights over every child who receives adoption. Paul makes it wonderfully clear that our heavenly Father adopted us with rejoicing not reluctance. In Ephesians 1:4–5 he says, 'In love he predestined us to be adopted… *in accordance with his pleasure and will.*'

Please note that word 'pleasure'. Our Father chose to adopt us not just because it was his sovereign will, but also because it was his special pleasure. It pleased him to enfold us in the eternal family of faith. It brought him joy and thrilled his heart. Even though this adoption would not be cost-free, God did not undertake this task by gritting his teeth and clenching his fists. No, it was his pleasure as well as his will.

As with Philip and Joy Stibbe, the Father's desire to adopt was motivated not only by decision but by delight! When my adoptive father looked at Claire and me in that orphanage in London, he not only decided to adopt us, it also pleased him to adopt us. Indeed, all through my life, he constantly stressed that he was overjoyed with that decision. Even when I was behaving in an ungracious way, he constantly emphasized that he never regretted adopting us. My abiding memory of the man I am pleased to call my father is this: that he was immensely pleased with his decision to adopt.

When I think back to those days in that orphanage in Hackney, I am overwhelmed with a sense of gratitude that Philip and Joy Stibbe decided to adopt my sister and me. We might have never left that place. Or we might have been parted from each other. Worse still, we could have ended up in an environment that encouraged us to live a life of crime. When I think of the diverse routes my life might have taken, I am so grateful for the undeserved love of my adoptive parents, Philip and Joy. They have rescued me from so much grief, and they have brought me so many privileges.

Writing this reminds me of the crucial theme of 'grace' in these verses in Ephesians 1. Paul is at pains to remind us that God adopted us as his sons 'to the praise of his glorious grace, which he has freely given us in the One he loves'.

A few words later, he says that our redemption through the blood of Jesus, the forgiveness of our sins, was 'in accordance with the riches of God's grace that he lavished on us with all wisdom and understanding'.

We did not deserve to be adopted, but then the abiding quality in the Father-heart of God is 'grace', or 'unearned love'. Our heavenly Father delights in *lavishing* his love on us. This is his will *and his pleasure*. That thought alone should release a constant flow of gratitude from our lips. Think what you might have been if you had not been adopted. Consider what you have been rescued from! Then pour out your praise in the words of 1 John 3:1:

How great is the love the Father has lavished on us, that we should be called children of God!

THE FATHER'S PERFECTION

How important it is to have a biblical image of God! Many people's picture of God is distorted because of wrong theology. This wrong theology may be caused by a lack of the word in a person's life. It is equally likely to be caused by a lack of the Spirit. As I shall show later on in this book, a person whose view of God is based on what the word says will have a healthy view of God as the most wonderful Father. As that person continues to walk in the Spirit, the Holy Spirit will also saturate the spirit of that person, bringing a constant inner witness that God is their Father and that they are beloved children of God.

If we're honest, though, our image of God is coloured by our own fathers. Those who have had absent or cruel fathers tend to find it hard to believe in the perfection of God's fatherly love. Those who have had good fathers tend to find it a lot easier. Speaking for myself, I am one of those strange people who have had two fathers. My first father abandoned me at birth. I never knew him. I don't even know his name. My second father—Philip Stibbe, the man I am pleased to call my real father—adopted me. He was as near to a perfect father as one could meet. He was extraordinarily accepting of my sister and me, and looked upon us with the same pleasure that he had for his own, natural son,

Giles. He lavished undeserved love upon us, and made us feel 'included' (Ephesians 1:13).

When my adoptive father died on 17 January 1997, the whole family was heart-broken. Yet his memorial service in Norwich Cathedral was a triumphant celebration of a life lived to the full—a life lived God's way. My father was a committed Christian. He had been converted as an Oxford undergraduate as a result of a conversation on a train with a well-known evangelical bishop. Subsequently, he lived his life in tune with the kingdom values of Jesus and, as a teacher and then a headmaster, sought to impart this faith to the pupils he taught. Just a month ago I was impressed again by the truth of this statement. I had just finished a workshop about the Father-heart of God. I had made mention of how my adoptive father had helped me to cultivate a healthy image of God's fatherhood. An elderly gentleman came up to me at the end of the session and said these words:

I agree totally with everything you have said about your father. He was one of three men in the entire course of my life who has made a genuine impression on me. I was a boy at Bradfield College when your dad was a teacher there. I had lost my own dad. Your father cared for me like a father. He was truly a father to the fatherless.

When the time came for my father's memorial service at Norwich Cathedral, I was asked to read from the scriptures. When my brother Giles and I searched through Dad's things before the service, we found a notebook of his. The notes began with the statement that he didn't actually want a service at all—which was typical of the man's integrity and humility. But he then went on to say that if the family insisted, then he wanted certain things in it. The one scripture reading he wanted was from Luke 15, the Parable of the Prodigal Son.

When I stood to read in that great cathedral, I felt led to say the following words of introduction:

Before I read the passage which my father himself requested for this service, I'd like to say something about the passage itself.

I would like to say that this well-known parable from Luke's Gospel is a most fitting passage for me to read today. In the English translations of the New Testament, this passage is given the title, 'The Parable of the Prodigal Son'. In the original Greek manuscripts, however, there are no titles, no chapter or verse numbers. There are merely paragraphs of Greek prose—known as pericopae—without any verbal or numerical headings.

I don't know who first gave this narrative the title, 'The Parable of the Prodigal Son', but, whoever it was, it was a mixed blessing. Yes, one of the protagonists in the story is certainly the wayward son who—in the immortal words of Adrian Plass—turns from affluent to effluent! But there is another character who is equally important. I am referring to the father who, with tear-soaked eyes, bade farewell to his younger son, and then waited daily at the village gates, in the frail hope of his son's return.

Let me say that this parable would lose nothing if our English translations entitled it, 'The Parable of the Perfect Father'. For one of Jesus' intentions was surely to show, through the character of the forgiving and demonstrative father, something of the God whom Jesus revealed as 'Our Father'. Perhaps the greatest compliment I can pay to my own dad, as we meet to remember him today, is this: that he, like the father in the story, has always been, and will always be, a window on to the Father-heart of God.

If you think about it, all earthly fathers are supposed to be windows on to the Father-heart of God. This is why Paul says in Ephesians 3:14, 'For this reason I bow the knee before the Father, from whom all fatherhood in heaven and on earth derives its name.'

Yet so many believers today find that their image of God is coloured by their painful experiences of their own father. In a later chapter I will show how my experience of being abandoned by my first father adversely affected my walk with God. I will demonstrate from my own story how easy it is to be misled into a false picture of the Father by looking at him through the spectacles of our childhood pain. But the good news of my testimony is this: that we can be healed of all that and come to a place where our old image goes and a new, wholesome picture of God replaces it. In my own life I have made a journey from one image of God to another—from an image based on my experience of being abandoned by my natural father, to an image based on the word of God and the revelation of the Holy Spirit. In moving to an image of God as a perfect, adopting Father, the example of Philip Stibbe has been of critical importance.

The truth is, believers were predestined for adoption as sons and daughters! We have a perfect Father who adopts us, loves us, and cares about us passionately. This is not just my own personal testimony. This is the testimony of both the word and the Spirit. As you learn to celebrate your adoption, learn to celebrate the perfect Fatherhood of God. There is no one as perfect as he is. Even my own dad would have shuddered at the thought of being described as 'perfect'. He was very conscious of his inadequacies as a husband and as a father. He would no doubt be horrified at the thought of his son's adulation of him! But our heavenly Abba is in an altogether different category. Of him the word 'perfection' can truly be used. As Jesus said, 'Be perfect, therefore, as your heavenly Father is perfect' (Matthew 5:48).

THE FATHER'S PURITY

Many of us sigh when we hear this command to be perfect. We wonder how we will ever achieve the same quality of holiness that God possesses. Surely we will never attain the Father's level of purity. Surely we will always have to settle for a less-than-perfect standard in this life, and at the same time hope that we will do enough to be made perfect in the life to come.

Yet Paul says in Ephesians 1 that we were chosen and adopted 'to be holy and blameless in God's sight' (v. 4). There is a goal to our adoption, and this has to do with being 'chips off the old block'—being like our Father in heaven. Jesus' teaching in the Sermon on the Mount, which is primarily about Christian conduct, proves the point. Sons imitate their fathers. As Jesus says of our attitude towards our persecutors: 'Love your enemies and pray for those who persecute you, that you may be sons of your Father in heaven' (Matthew 5:44–45). Being holy and blameless is therefore proof of our sonship.

What does it mean to be 'holy and blameless'? 'Holy' means 'separate from the world'. It denotes a life of moral purity that stands out in an immoral age. 'Blameless' means without defect. Like the lambs slaughtered at Passover (none of whose bones were to be broken), it denotes the absence of any hidden imperfections. 'Holy and blameless' therefore means 'living life the Father's way and free from every fault'. In Ephesians 5:27, Paul uses this same pair of words when he paints a picture of the church as the radiant bride of Christ, 'without stain or wrinkle or any other blemish, but *holy* and *blameless*'.

How can we ever be holy and blameless? At this point I want to stress again the importance of Paul's concept of adoption. As I wrote in the first chapter, adoption has been the most neglected doctrine in the church. Since the Reformation, there has been considerable emphasis upon justi-fication by faith, and rightly so. As Packer says, it is 'the foundational blessing of the gospel'. But apart from theologians who have emerged in times of revival (such as Wesley, Edwards and Spurgeon), there has been an almost total neglect of the 'highest blessing of the gospel', namely our adoption.

What happens to believers who know they are justified, but who have no real sense in their hearts that they are adopted by a perfect Father? The consequences are severe. Believers who have no doctrine or experience of adoption will basically relate to God as Master but not as Father. They will be in a Master–servant rather than a Father–son relationship with God. They will know that they are justified by their faith in the unmerited love of God at Calvary, but until they know their adoption they will always see God as a Master who must be obeyed rather than a Father whom one would never want to grieve. In other words, they will live as slaves rather than sons. They will be subject to the love of law rather than the law of love.

Let me put it this way: the father who adopted me was a fine man. Of all the people I have met in my life, Philip Stibbe is the man I have most admired. His values were Christian, his life was holy, and his bearing impressive. My father was not a man who wielded an iron rod over my life, a remote and angry figure who wanted me to do as I was told. Far from it! He was a close and gentle father whose affection inspired obedience. As I grew up, my motivation for behaving well was therefore not fear but love. I tried to behave well because I didn't want to jeopardize the intimacy of my relationship with my dad. I didn't want to do anything which might make him grow distant.

Now there's an interesting grammatical point concerning Ephesians 1:4–5 which may help us to see the importance of this in relation to our Father in heaven. This revolves around the words 'in love'. The NIV translates these verses as follows:

For he chose us in him before the creation of the world to be holy and blameless in his sight. In love he predestined us to be adopted as his sons...

According to this translation, the words 'in love' describe the Father's reason for adopting us. They refer to what I earlier called 'the Father's Passion'. However, the Authorised Version, Revised Version and the New English Bible translate these verses differently. They put the words 'in love' at the end of the sentence about being holy and blameless:

For he chose us in him before the creation of the world to be holy and blameless in love. He predestined us to be adopted as his sons...

If we take the second translation as correct, then Paul is saying that it is only in a relationship of love between us and our heavenly Father that a holy and a blameless life can be lived. It is only amongst those who know they are adopted sons and daughters, and who are living in an attitude of joyful gratitude for this fact, that true purity of life can be attained. Those who know they are loved by the Father, and who reciprocate that love, choose to be holy because they are passionate about God. They live blameless lives because the fire of God's love burns within their hearts and they don't want to quench that fire in any way. Put another way, all earthly passions are eclipsed by the heavenly passion that flows between the believer and the Father.

I am not a Greek specialist so I cannot tell you which translation is correct (though Bible teachers such as John Stott argue that 'in love' should be taken with 'holy and blameless'). But if this second rendering of these verses is the right one, then it reveals how important adoption is to the whole matter of sanctification. Sanctification is the lifelong process of growing towards moral perfection. It is the process by which we become more and more like our Father. It seems to me that a person who does not truly know God as Father will always find it hard to live a holy and blameless life. Such a person will see God as a Master who must be obeyed rather than a Father whose loving acceptance inspires obedience. He will live like a slave rather than a son. He will know that he is justified, but having failed to enter into the fullness of his adoption through the power of the Spirit, he will always find it hard to be fully motivated for holiness.

This, then, is the reason why Paul connects our spiritual adoption with the goal of holiness in Ephesians 1:4–5. The sad truth, however, is that many Christians have failed to see the link. They do not see the three links in the chain of our growth as Christians. These three links comprise Justification (getting right with the Father), Adoption (becoming a son of the Father) and Sanctification (becoming more and more like the Father):

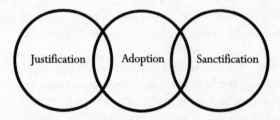

In an ideal scenario, a person becomes justified before God through faith in the saving efficacy of the death of Jesus. At this stage, his spirituality is one in which God is very much the Almighty and all-seeing Judge. The Spirit at work within him is the Spirit who convicts us of our guilt in relation to sin, righteousness and judgment, and who enables us to confess Jesus as Lord. However, this same Spirit is also called 'the Spirit of adoption'. This Spirit is not just the refining fire of God's holiness. He is the fire of God's love. As the new believer becomes more and more filled with this Spirit, the 'Abba' cry is released from his heart. He rejoices that the Father himself loves him, that he is accepted and cherished by the Father, and that he is an adopted son of God. As this knowledge deepens, so the new believer delights to say 'yes' to the call of holiness upon his life. Far from being driven by whips, the adopted child of God is drawn by cords of love into a place of deeper and deeper consecration. At every stage of the journey, therefore (justification, adoption, and sanctification), the disciple of Jesus is led by the Spirit not driven by the flesh.

Now see what happens when the doctrine and experience of adoption is left out of the picture. Instead of being drawn by cords of love, the believer is driven by whips of self-effort. Instead of seeing God as a Father whose affection inspires obedience, he sees God as a Judge who is ready to condemn or a Master who demands obedience:

THE ADOPTION GAP

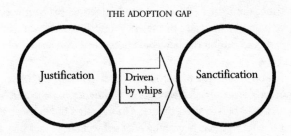

This, in short, is the difference between living like a slave and living like a son. The first sees God as a perfectionist slave-driver who drives us towards holiness with whips of 'ought' and 'must'. The second sees God as a perfect Father who draws us towards holiness with cords of love. Perhaps you can now see why neglecting our spiritual adoption has severe consequences for those who want to be 'holy and blameless'. Instead of saying 'I want to be holy', the person with no revelation of the Father-heart of God says, 'I must be holy'. Instead of being led by the Spirit into deeper levels of the Father's purity, this person is driven by the flesh with ever-increasing guilt and shame. His motivation to be holy is a Pharisaic one.

Brennan Manning has expressed this point in a helpful analogy. He compares the obedience of an unloved child with the obedience of a child that has known a lot of love:

Suppose a child has never experienced any love from her parents. One day she meets another little girl whose parents shower her with affection. The first says to herself: 'I want to be loved like that too. I have never experienced it, but I'm going to earn the love of my mother and father by my good behaviour.' So to gain the affection of her parents, she brushes her teeth, makes her bed, smiles, minds her p's and q's, never pouts or cries, never expresses a need, and conceals negative feelings. This is the way of the Pharisees. They follow the law impeccably in order to induce God's love... In sharp contrast to the Pharisaic perception of God and religion, the Biblical perception of the gospel of grace is that of a child who has never experienced anything but love and who tries to do her best because she is loved.[21]

Paul says that the Father chose and predestined us for adoption as sons so that we might be holy and blameless. In other words, God adopted us so that we would exhibit the family likeness. He chose us in order that we would live a life in which his purity was clearly visible. Those who constantly know God in a Master–servant relationship (or, even a Judge–defendant relationship) will always have a tendency to be driven by whips when it comes to personal obedience. On the other hand, those in whom the Spirit of adoption has been fully released will know that they are sons and daughters of a perfect Father; for them, personal obedience will be much more a matter of being drawn by cords of love.

THE GLORIOUS FATHER

Anyone who cultivates an image of God based on the first chapter of Ephesians will have a truly magnificent picture of God. This is a Father who has blessed us with every spiritual blessing (v. 3), chosen us before the foundation of the world (v. 4), predestined us for adoption as sons and daughters (v. 5), redeemed and forgiven us (v. 7), lavished the riches of his grace upon us (v. 8), made known to us the mystery of his great plan for the universe (v. 9), included us in this plan (v. 13), and marked us with the seal of his promised Holy Spirit (v. 13). No wonder Paul describes God as 'the *glorious* Father' in Ephesians 1:17.

What kind of father did you have? In the two columns below you will find contrasting qualities associated with fathers. As you read down the list, consider which of these words describes your own father:

unconditionally loving	conditionally loving
good at communicating	poor at communicating
releasing	controlling
understanding	judgmental
trustworthy	unreliable
self-controlled	out of control
outgoing	introverted
warm and affectionate	cold and aloof
self-respecting	self-hating
accepting	critical
sensitive	indifferent
available	absent
honest	dishonest
protective	abusive
forgiving	unforgiving
generous	stingy
playful	non-playful

All the characteristics on the left-hand side describe aspects of the Fatherhood of God. If Paul were with us right now, he would say that the reason for this is grace. What is grace? Philip Yancey defines it in these great words:

Grace means that there is nothing we can do to make God love us more... There is nothing we can do to make God love us less. [22]

It is truly a life-changing thing to recognize that our God is a gracious, generous and glorious Father. He is a Father who is always understanding, trustworthy and available. He is never physically or emotionally absent. He has promised not to leave or forsake us. He is forever affectionate and affirming, protective and forgiving. As we saw in the last chapter, he even rejoices over us with singing!

CHAPTER 4

The Son who Became a Slave

Let me introduce you to my older brother Giles. He is two and a half years older than me and is the only natural, biological child of Philip and Joy Stibbe (who adopted me). Over the years he has grown more and more like his father. He looks like Dad—a full head of black hair, slightly crooked nose, same height. He sounds like Dad—indeed, people often used to mistake him for my father when he answered the telephone. Like Dad, Giles has an extraordinarily generous spirit and is respected by everyone. Today he is a major in the Life Guards and is stationed near Windsor Castle. On at least one occasion he has been invited to have dinner with the royal family. Giles is a man I greatly love and admire. I am touched that he regards me as his brother, and I am honoured to be in his family.

When Dad died in January 1997, our relationship with him was obviously ended. He was gone from our lives. We couldn't speak with him any more. We couldn't be in his presence any more. The joy of his company was now lost to us. In a strange way, however, my absent father is still with me. My brother Giles is so much like Dad that he is a constant reminder of what my father looked like and the kind of man my father was. I can see so many of my dad's mannerisms in Giles that it is sometimes just like being in my father's presence. Giles is like a living likeness of my father's character. The way he speaks to me, the way he behaves towards me, is a constant reflection of Dad's greatest virtues. I can pay Giles no greater compliment than that.

THE FATHER'S REFLECTION

In the Book of Hebrews, the writer says that Jesus is 'the radiance of God's glory, the exact representation of God's being' (Hebrews 1:3). Jesus is the Son who reflects the glory of the Father. He is a window on to the Father. As he himself said to the apostle Philip:

Don't you know me, Philip, even after I have been among you such a long time? Anyone who has seen me has seen the Father. How can you say, 'Show us the Father?' Don't you believe that I am in the Father, and that the Father is in me? The words I say to you are not just my own. Rather, it is the Father, living in me, who is doing his work.
JOHN 14:9–10

If we want to know what our Father in heaven is like, then we need to look at Jesus. Jesus is the human face of Yahweh. He is the living likeness of God the Father. Just as Giles is a constant reminder to me of my adoptive father, so Jesus is an exact reflection of our Father in heaven. He is the radiance of the Father's glory. He who has met Jesus, has met the Father.

How can this be? At this point we need to take seriously a word that is used on two occasions in John's Gospel. On each occasion it is used of Jesus. That word is, in the Greek, *monogenes*, meaning 'one and only', or 'one of a kind':

The Word became flesh and made his dwelling among us. We have seen his glory, the glory of the One and Only [monogenes], who came from the Father, full of grace and truth.
JOHN 1:14

For God so loved the world that he gave his one and only [monogenes] Son, that whoever believes in him shall not perish but have eternal life.
JOHN 3:16

These statements show that Jesus Christ was God's one and only Son by nature. He was not an adopted son. The idea that Jesus was adopted into sonship is the essential error within the heresy known as 'adoptionism', associated with Paul of Samosata and two men called Theodotus.[23] They believed that Jesus was adopted as the Son of God when the Spirit descended upon him at his baptism in the River Jordan. Part of the reasoning behind this is the fact that the Father quotes from Psalm 2:7 when the heavens are torn open. The heavenly voice says, 'You are my Son.' The full statement from Psalm 2 is, 'You are my Son, today I have begotten you.' Some ancient manuscripts of Luke's story of Jesus' baptism even have the second phrase, 'Today I have begotten you', included. But for some even the first part of the quotation was enough to indicate that Jesus was adopted as Son at his baptism. For them, the day of his baptism was the day on which he was begotten as Son.

However, the scriptures do not permit us to go in this direction. The New Testament makes it crystal clear that Jesus was God's Son from eternity to eternity. At the beginning of John, Jesus is described as the eternal Word:

In the beginning was the Word, and the Word was with God, and the Word was God. He was with God in the beginning.
JOHN 1:1–2

And Jesus can say in John 17:5:

And now Father, glorify me in your presence with the glory I had with you before the world began.

This helps us to understand why Jesus can be called *monogenes* ('one of a kind'). As Origen insisted, 'Jesus does not become Son in an external way through the adoption of the Spirit, but is Son by nature' (*De Principiis* 1.2.4). Jesus Christ existed from eternity in a relationship of unparalleled intimacy with God the Father (John 1:18). This means that Jesus of Nazareth is far more than a great teacher, far more than a great prophet, far more than a great leader, far more than a great moralist. Jesus Christ is the Son of God, the Second Person of the Trinity, the One and Only of God.

Here again my own family history is helpful. Giles is the natural son of Philip and Joy Stibbe. Claire and I are children by adoption. The difference between my sonship and Giles' is the difference between transferred and inherent sonship. My sonship is transferred via the legal rite of adoption. Giles' is inherent; he is a son 'by nature'. Therefore, of Giles it can be said that he is the one and only of his parents. While Claire and I know that we are special to our parents, our filial status is different from Giles'.

While Christians 'become' sons through regeneration and adoption (John 1:12–13), Jesus is always a Son. Indeed, he has always been God's Son, and always will be God's Son. God ceases truly to be God once you take Jesus, his Son, out of the picture. If you remove us, however, God does not cease to be God. The baptism of Jesus was therefore not an adoption into sonship but an affirmation of existing sonship. Jesus was God's Son from eternity to eternity. As Origen put it, Jesus stands 'always in uninterrupted contemplation of the depths of the Father' (*Commentary on John* 2.2.18).

ABBA, FATHER

One of the proofs of Jesus' unique filial relationship with the Father is his constant use of the phrase 'Father' when addressing God. In the Old Testament, the revelation of the Fatherhood of God is partially concealed. In the New Testament, 'Father' is shown to be the Christian name of God. Jesus' theology is a Father-shaped theology. The word he used to describe God was 'Abba'. As Joachim Jeremias' classic study of this word has shown:

- This was an intimate form of address used by children in an Aramaic-speaking home. Children would address their mothers as 'imma' and their fathers as 'abba'.
- Jesus' use of this word in his relationship with God was unique in Judaism.
- His use of this word with reference to God discloses the unique nature of his filial relationship with God.
- Jesus taught his own followers to address God as 'Our Father in heaven', thereby inviting them into the same intimate relationship with God that he knew.[24]

Recent studies of the word 'father' prior to and contemporary with Jesus have tried to destroy Jeremias' position. The discovery of a few religious examples of the use of the word 'father' have been used to suggest that Jesus' use of 'Abba' was distinctive rather than absolutely unique. In additon to this, some have tried to show that the word 'Abba' was not the equivalent of 'Daddy' and that it therefore cannot be used as evidence of Jesus' intimate relationship with God. The chief reason for saying this is the discovery that the word 'Abba' was used by Jewish adults of their fathers.[25]

It is now clear that these criticisms have gone too far. While it is agreed that the use of the word 'Abba' was not *unique* to Jesus, it is generally felt that it was distinctive of him. No one else used this term so frequently of God. Furthermore, while 'Daddy' may not be a perfect translation of 'Abba' ('Papa' is probably the nearest English equivalent), the argument that it does *not* denote intimacy has been called into question. The fact that adults used 'Abba' when they spoke to their earthly fathers is no argument at all. Many adults, even in an English-speaking culture, still refer to their fathers as 'Dad' or 'Daddy'. As Gordon Fee writes, 'that it was used by adult children as well as small children is irrelevant'. He concludes:

If 'Daddy' is not an exact equivalent—and it is not—the basic thrust of the term, and the exact significance of Jesus' use of it in addressing God, nevertheless carries considerable theological weight. If the term cannot be demonstrated, as Jeremias supposed, to be unique to Jesus, it can surely be argued that it was distinctively his form of address; and for Jesus it is best understood as a term denoting his own sense of unique Sonship—by addressing God consistently in the language of the home.[26]

Throughout the Gospels, Jesus addresses God as 'Father', and this fact alone demonstrates his unique relationship with God. The sheer number of these references is itself overwhelming evidence that Jesus must have used 'Abba' in his private prayer and public teaching:[27]

	MARK	LUKE	MATTHEW	JOHN
'Father'	3	4	31	100
'The Father'	1	2	1	73

Some sceptical scholars claim that the greatest number of these references occurs in John's Gospel and that they therefore cannot prove the case at all—because John is the least historical of the Gospels. This, however, is mistaken. We find Jesus speaking in the Synoptic Gospels in a way that is similar to the way he speaks in John. Take Luke 10:22 (paralleled in Matthew 11:27) as an example:

All things have been committed to me by my Father. No one knows who the Son is except the Father, and no one knows who the Father is except the Son and those to whom the Son chooses to reveal him.

Liberal scholars have always been embarrassed by this saying. To them it sounds far too like the Jesus of John's Gospel—a Jesus whom they dismiss as unhistorical. Indeed, they refer to Jesus' language here as an asteroid from the Johannine sky! To any reasonable person, however, these words sound so close to John's Gospel because this is how the historical Jesus actually spoke about God and about himself! The truth is, Jesus enjoyed a unique filial relationship with God the Father. Jesus' remarks in Luke 10 and Matthew 11, along with all his talk about the Fatherhood of God in John, reflect the certain historical fact of Jesus' special intimacy with the Living God. At least at one point in the Gospels, the Evangelists even preserve the original Aramaic word that Jesus actually used (Mark 14:35–36):

Going a little farther, he fell to the ground and prayed that if possible the hour might pass from him. 'Abba, Father', he said, 'everything is possible for you. Take this cup from me. Yet not what I will, but what you will.'

THE SON WHO BECAME A SLAVE

I have said in an earlier chapter that the purpose of Jesus' life and ministry is inextricably bound up with our spiritual adoption. I expressed it this way: *the Son became a slave that we, who were slaves, might become sons.*[28] Paul, in his letter to the Philippians, says that Jesus, 'being in very nature God, did not consider equality with God something to be grasped, but

made himself nothing, taking the very nature of a slave [doulos]'
(Philippians 2:6–7). Here Paul emphasizes that Jesus was in very nature
God. He did not become divine, he has always been divine. He was not
adopted as a Son. He was the eternal Son of God by nature.

At the same time, Paul says that Jesus did not count equality with God
something to be clung on to possessively. Rather, he emptied himself and
humbled himself. He left the majesty of heaven, the glory of eternity, the
privileges of divinity, in order to be born as a baby in Bethlehem. He lived
a life of total obedience to the will of God and as such became a noble
slave to the perfect plan of God. He told those around him that he had
come not to be served but to serve and to give his life as a ransom for
many. At the end of his life, he fulfilled the prophecy of the Suffering
Servant in Isaiah 53 and died in our place on the cross. Truly, the Son
became a slave that we who were slaves might become sons. This is
indeed good news. As Packer puts it:

It is like a fairy story—the reigning monarch adopts waifs and strays to
make princes of them—but, praise God, it is not a fairy story: it is hard
and solid fact...[29]

For Paul, there are at least two extraordinary things about Jesus' life on
earth. The first is the fact that he became a doulos, a slave, for our sakes.
He did not arrive as the King of Kings, with myriads of heralds, and
unavoidable publicity. He came as the Servant of Yahweh, the noble slave
of God's will. Secondly, he came to die on the cross. Paul was a Roman
citizen, and he knew that crucifixion was the form of execution reserved
for slaves.[30] Crucifixion was called servile supplicium (the slaves' punishment). Slaves were crucified outside Jerusalem as they were outside every
major city in the Roman Empire. After the defeat of Spartacus, six
thousand of them were crucified on the Appian Way between Rome and
Capua. The life of a slave in the Roman Empire was therefore extremely
precarious. Seneca says that Roman slaves lived sub certo crucis periculo,
under the certain threat of crucifixion.

Paul writes that Jesus took the form of a slave and became obedient to
death on a cross. For Paul's addressees the implication is clear: Jesus

became the lowest form of life in the Roman Empire, a slave. More than that, he died by crucifixion—the *servile supplicium*, the slaves' punishment. Jesus Christ lived the life of a slave and he died the death of a slave. Something of this is implied when he washes the disciples' feet at the Last Supper. Washing feet was something required of a Roman slave (though interestingly not of a Jewish slave). Jesus performs this menial task to show that he had come to live and die as a slave. Why? So that we who were spiritually enslaved might become the adopted sons and daughters of the High King of Heaven. So that we who are spiritually impure might be washed clean and reconciled to Abba, Father.

Out of the Orphanage

At the Last Supper (the same meal at which he performs the duties of a Roman slave), Jesus makes a beautiful promise—one which highlights the fact that he had come to turn slaves into sons. On the night before he dies, Jesus says, 'I will not leave you as orphans' (John 14:18). During the Last Supper, Jesus is acutely conscious that his disciples will be left bereft and heartbroken the next day. They will feel very much alone once he has died on the cross. So here, in John 14, he promises that he will give them the Holy Spirit after he has departed. By this same Spirit, the Father and the Son will make their homes in the lives of all obedient believers (John 14:23). Once Jesus has left them to return to the Father, he will give his followers 'Abba's perfect present'. This is the promised gift of the Holy Spirit (Acts 1:4). Those who believe in him will no longer be orphans—spiritually homeless in the universe—but will receive the Spirit of adoption. Then they too will cry out 'Abba, Father' to God. For this to happen, however, Jesus must first die a slave's death at Calvary.

Let's return at this point to the Roman practice of adoption. In the Roman rite, the child of a slave is under his natural father's authority. At a set price of gold or silver, this child is bought out of slavery by the adopting father. At that moment, the slave's debts are cancelled, he is declared *sui heredes* (the adopting father's heir) and is given a new family, a new fortune and a new future. Set free as he is from the *patria potestas* of his old father, he now has a new identity, new privileges and a new purpose. He has truly been delivered from slavery and adopted into sonship.

As I indicated in Chapter 2, the New Testament writers found 'adoption' a powerful image because they understood all too well that Jesus had paid the price for our emancipation on the cross. At Calvary, the full price for our adoption was paid. Two things therefore happened as a result of Jesus' Passion and death. First of all, we were delivered from the *patria potestas* of Satan. The cross is therefore a triumph not a tragedy. Through the power of the blood of Jesus, Satan's grip over our lives was loosened and our chains of slavery fell off. The cross is therefore the ultimate act of deliverance. It is the place where the prince of this world is driven out (John 12:31) and where Jesus is revealed as *Christus Victor*, Christ the Conqueror.

The second thing that happened as a result of the cross was that everything that was needed for our spiritual adoption was done in full. The redemption that was needed for us to become the adopted children of God was paid by Jesus. Something of this glorious work of adoption is made visible in a little incident just before Jesus' death. Looking down from the cross, Jesus sees his mother and the disciple whom he loved. To his mother he says, 'Dear woman, here is your son.' To his friend he says, 'Here is your mother.' This is perhaps the nearest thing in a Jewish context to a formal act of adoption.

Until we choose to believe in Jesus, we are slaves to sin and we are oppressed by what some call an 'orphan spirit'. That is why Jesus says to some of his Jewish contemporaries that they are slaves and that their father is the devil (John 8:31–47). Only through Jesus and his all-sufficient death on the cross can we be given our freedom. As Jesus says,

If you hold to my teaching, you are really my disciples. Then you will know the truth, and the truth will set you free.
John 8:31–32

The reason Jesus can tell his disciples that they will not be left as orphans is this: through the cross, they will receive deliverance from slavery and they will be adopted as sons. This is indeed cause for praise. As one hymn-writer (W.C. Dix) puts it:[31]

Alleluia! Not as orphans
Are we left in sorrow now;
Alleluia! He is near us,
Faith believes nor questions how.
Though the clouds from sight received Him
When the forty days were o'er,
Shall our hearts forget His promise,
'I am with you evermore'?

THE FIRSTBORN AMONG MANY BROTHERS

On the cross, Jesus pays the price for our deliverance from slavery and for our adoption as sons. But the story doesn't end there. Jesus' body lay in the tomb of Joseph of Arimathea for three days (according to the Jewish reckoning of time). On the third day, Death gave up its futile attempt to hold on to him, and God sent grave-busting, death-destroying power from heaven into the sinless body of the crucified Messiah. Jesus was raised as the firstborn among many brothers. In the process, Jesus blazed a trail from earth to heaven and opened up the way to the Father's house. Many sons and daughters can now be led on this road to glory. Those who love Jesus can now be set free from the slavery of the fear of death and follow their Brother to Abba's house (Hebrews 2:10–18).

This means that the New Testament doesn't only regard the cross as pivotal for our adoption. The resurrection is pivotal too. What is the evidence for this? When Jesus is raised on the first Easter Sunday, he meets Mary Magdalene in the garden where the empty tomb was situated. Mary mistakes him for the gardener. He then speaks her name, and she recognizes him as Jesus, exclaiming, 'Rabboni', meaning 'My Master'. Jesus then gives Mary the following task (John 20:17):

Go to my brothers and tell them, 'I am returning to my Father and your Father, to my God and your God.'

Origen regarded this as the key moment in John's Gospel. He argued that until Jesus' death and resurrection, the disciples related to God in a Master–servant manner. They were the servants of their rabbi Jesus and they were, through him, the servants of God. Now, however, Jesus' death and resurrection have opened up a new and better way of relating to God. Now the disciples can relate to God as 'Father'. That is why Jesus says to Mary, 'I am returning to my Father and *your* Father'. Furthermore, the disciples no longer relate to Jesus merely as 'Rabbi' or even 'Rabboni'. Now they can call Jesus 'brother'. That is why Jesus says, 'Go and tell the *brothers*' the good news of the resurrection. For Origen, the resurrection is therefore as important as the cross in establishing a new, Father–son relationship for us. The old Master–servant relationship has been super-seded by a more intimate, filial and altogether relational walk with God. Disciples can now relate to God with filial love rather than servile fear. That is why Jesus says in John 15:15:

I no longer call you servants [douloi], because a servant does not know his master's business. Instead, I have called you friends, for everything that I learned from my Father I have made known to you.

The resurrection is therefore as important as the cross. Jesus is truly the firstborn among many brothers. He is the brother who said, 'I'll go ahead of you into the valley of the shadow of death. But don't worry. On the third day I'm going to rise again and what happens to me will happen to you when your time comes. Indeed, I will come back and take you to be with me in the Father's house.' If God is our perfect, glorious Father, then Jesus is our perfect, older Brother, for what other man has ever done something like this for his brothers and sisters? Truly, there is no one like Jesus. He is indeed 'the One and Only of God'.

The perfect older brother

The idea that Jesus is our Brother is one of the most neglected ideas in the doctrine of Christ. Jesus is often portrayed as Friend, Saviour, Lord, King, Healer, Spirit-baptizer, Sanctifier, and so on. The idea that he is also our brother is strangely ignored. This could be because it makes Jesus sound too familiar. It could also be because a lot of theologians have had problems in their relationships with their brothers! Whatever the case, it is supremely important for us to recover this rich image of Jesus. In the New Testament, it is perfectly clear that there is only one way to know God intimately as Father, and that is by becoming the best friends of his one and only Son. Jesus is the way to the Father, the truth about the Father, and the life of the Father. No one comes to the Father except through him (John 14:6).

A lovely story is told about a young soldier during the American Civil War. He was desperate to have a private interview with Abraham Lincoln, the President of the United States. He tried to get into the White House to see him, but was refused admission. So he sat outside looking forlorn and dejected. A young man saw him there and went and sat with him.

'What's the matter?' he asked.

'I need to see the President,' he replied.

'Why?' asked the young man.

'Because I need to be excused military service. Both my parents are seriously ill and I must go home to look after them.'

'Come with me,' said the man, and he led the soldier back into the White House, past all the guards and the statesmen, into the Oval Office where Abraham Lincoln was seated.

'What can I do for you, Todd?' said the President to the young man who had escorted the soldier.

'Dad, this man is a soldier. He has a serious problem and he needs to see you for a few minutes.'

I love this story not only because it is true but also because it highlights the fact that we cannot have access to the Father except through the Son. If you and I want to enjoy intimacy with God, then it has to be through Jesus. If we want to enjoy the full liberty of our status as adopted children of God, then it has to be through the Son by nature. God has not given any other means by which he may be known personally. We come to the Father via the Brother.

At the beginning of this chapter I wrote about my adoptive father, Philip Stibbe. I mentioned how important Giles is because he is the reflection of my father. He is a window on to my father who is now in heaven. Without Giles, my image of my father would be fading fast. My memories of him would be starting to go. When I am with Giles, however, a picture of my father's face returns. My memory of his voice is restored. The more I spend time with my brother, the more I can recall the man who was my father.

In a similar way, we cannot enter into the full joy of intimacy with Abba, Father unless we spend time with our perfect Brother Jesus. This is why it is so important to recover what we might call a 'Brother Christology'—an understanding of Christ founded on the Brotherhood of Jesus. In a passage that has become much loved to me, we learn the following:

Both the one who makes men holy and those who are made holy are of the same family. So Jesus is not ashamed to call them brothers. He says, 'I will declare your name to my brothers; in the presence of the congregation I will sing your praises.' And again, 'I will put my trust in him.' And again he says, 'Here am I, and the children God has given me.'
HEBREWS 2:11–13

Here the author of Hebrews shows us that Jesus is in the same family as we are, that he is delighted to regard us as his brothers and sisters, and that he declares God's name to us as we gather together in worship.

In Chapters 2 and 3, I mentioned how important Zephaniah 3:17 has become to many believers in recent years. There God is portrayed as a Father who rejoices over us with singing. In these verses in Hebrews 2:11–13, another side to this remarkable truth is revealed. As the Father rejoices over us with singing, the Son rejoices over the Father with singing. As the Father rejoices over his adopted sons and daughters in song, our Brother Jesus sings joyfully about the Father, and presents himself and us to God.

What is the song that Jesus sings as we gather to worship God? The writer to the Hebrews says that Jesus declares God's name to his brothers and sisters. What is the name of God? It is surely the name that Jesus used in his own devotional life and which he came to teach us in the

Lord's Prayer. It is the name, Abba, meaning 'Papa' or 'Dad'. True worship therefore happens when we join in with the singing Saviour. It is not just a matter of hearing the Father's song over us. It is also a matter of hearing the Son's song about the Father and joining in with that. As the revelation of the Father's delight over us comes from heaven to earth, so the song of the Son's delight goes from earth to heaven. What this means is that Jesus stands among us as our Risen Brother when we worship. The 'real presence' of the Risen Jesus is therefore known not just in the breaking of bread nor just in the ministry of the Word. It is also known in the supernatural refrains of the Melodious Messiah as he celebrates in song the many-splendoured thing that is the love of God. What a tragic thing it is that so many believers have never understood this wonderful truth because they have never experienced the loving Spirit of adoption.

THE NEED TO BE 'IN CHRIST'

Over the years there has been a great deal of emphasis in evangelical spirituality about the importance of 'Christ' being 'in me'. Evangelists have often seen the goal of their message as the appeal to sinners. This appeal consists of convincing people that they need to ask the Lord Jesus Christ to enter their lives as Saviour. There is nothing at all wrong with this. I have already mentioned a verse in John's Gospel which shows that the Father and the Son want to make their home in the hearts of believers (John 14:23). In Galatians 2:20 Paul says, 'Christ lives in me'. In Ephesians 3:17, Paul prays that Christ might take up permanent residence in us. So there is plenty of biblical warrant for this emphasis on 'Christ being in me' in evangelical spirituality. Indeed, it was this kind of preaching that led me to become a Christian and to enter into a personal relationship with the Lord Jesus myself.

At the same time, evangelical piety has often neglected the reverse of the equation, that being a Christian is a matter of 'me being in Christ'— or, better still, of us being in Christ. The idea of us being 'in Christ' is in fact far more common in the New Testament than the idea of Christ being in us. In Ephesians, Paul begins, 'Praise be to the God and Father of our Lord Jesus Christ, who has blessed us in the heavenly realms with every spiritual blessing *in Christ*' (1:3). This is the first time in the letter that Paul uses the expression, 'in Christ'. But in the next ten verses of this opening prayer he uses this (or a similar) expression eleven times in the Greek! Evidently Paul was very keen to get his readers to see the dynamic importance not only of Christ being in them but also of them being in Christ.

What does it mean to be 'in Christ'? It means to be joined to the Son's relationship with the Father through the power of the Holy Spirit. It means entering into that intimate, filial relationship that Jesus has with Abba, Father, through the Spirit. A true Christian is someone who has been incorporated through baptism into a community of adopted brothers and sisters. At the horizontal level, as it were, Christians are part of a community of people who used to be orphans but are now heirs, who used to be slaves but are now daughters and sons. All this is the work of the Holy Spirit who creates a *koinonia* or 'family-fellowship' of those who love their Brother Jesus.

At the vertical level, Christians are part of a community that is in an authentic relationship with the Risen Lord. We are part of a family that has been gathered by the Spirit into the Son's adoring love of the Father. To be 'in Christ' therefore means to be in charismatic fellowship with those who share in the Son's relationship with the Father. That is why Paul speaks with such trinitarian language of the believer's prayer life (in Romans 8). The believer begins by allowing the Holy Spirit, the Third Person of the Trinity, to pray through him with groans that words cannot express (Romans 8:26). The believer is then joined by the Spirit to the flow of intercession that is pouring from the heart of the Son of God, the Second Person of the Trinity (8:34). He is praying at the right hand of God the Father, the First Person of the Trinity. In Paul's mind, the reason why believers can pray in this way is simply because we are 'in Christ'. In other words, we have become part of the royal family of heaven as a result of believing the Son and receiving the loving Spirit of adoption.

That we are 'in Christ' from the moment we are born again is therefore a truth worth stressing. From now on, our prayer life is no longer a desperate struggle of the flesh. It is a matter of allowing the Holy Spirit to lift us on eagles' wings into that highest place where Jesus is pouring out his heart to the Father in loving adoration and in travailing prayer for the world. No one can attain these heights of intimacy and intercession unless they have first been adopted into the eternal family of heaven. Until a person is 'in Christ', they can never know the joy of being carried on the currents of the Spirit into the very heart of the Father's house. They can never know the privilege of entering the living room of heaven where the Father sings over his children and his children join in with Jesus in singing the praises of Abba, Father.

RESTING IN THE SPIRIT OF JESUS

If justification by faith is the foundational blessing of the gospel, spiritual adoption is the highest blessing. Through the adopting grace of the Father, the Son and the Holy Spirit, we can become 'like a little child before the good God' (Thérèse of Lisieux). We can become *ebro d'amore*, drunk with the Father's love (Catherine of Siena). This great privilege is not granted at the end of a process of frenetic activity, arduous ministry and constant self-effort. It is given by grace to those who enter the sabbath rest that Abba, Father grants to those who love his Son. This is why God's extravagant grace is always offensive to the Pharisee in us. The religious spirit demands that we live as slaves. The Holy Spirit woos us into resting in the Saviour's arms of love.

In the final analysis, the call of God upon our lives is to live as 'beloved disciples'. The beloved disciple is a character in John's Gospel who appears for the first time in John 13:23, resting 'on the bosom of Jesus'. This is almost exactly the same expression in the Greek as is used of Jesus in John 1:18, being 'in the bosom of the Father'. The implication of all this is clear. Those who rest in a place of intimacy with Jesus enter into that same intimate relationship which Jesus shares forever with the Father.

When was the last time you rested in the Spirit of Jesus? When was the last time you soaked in the intoxicating love of God? When was the last time you allowed the liquid waves of God's love to break upon you? The great theologian Edward Schillebeeckx wrote this, and I could never improve on it:

In a revealed religion, silence with God has a value in itself and for its own sake, just because God is God. Failure to recognize the value of mere being with God, as the beloved, without doing anything, is to gouge the heart out of Christianity.[32]

Jesus Christ, God's Son, became a slave, that we who were spiritually enslaved might become sons. Are we living like slaves or like sons? If we are living like slaves, then we will find resting in the Spirit of Jesus a great offence. If we are living as sons and daughters, then resting in the Spirit of Jesus will be the greatest delight. Living as slaves undermines the great and costly work of Jesus Christ. Living as sons and daughters shows that we have understood and truly valued that saving, adopting work. So which is it to be? Slavery or sonship?

CHAPTER 5

The Loving Spirit of Adoption

One of my lasting childhood memories is of my parents taking me to see the film, *The Railway Children*. Not long ago I watched it with my own children on TV, and the incident was re-lived. The story concerns a family in Victorian London. The father, a particularly loving, indeed doting, parent, is unjustly arrested and imprisoned. The mother then takes her children to live in the north of England. The rest of the story revolves around the three children and their adventures on a local steam railway line. Bobbie, the oldest child, manages to get a message to an elderly gentleman who travels on the same train every day. The message is a request for help in her father's release. At the end of the film (based on the 1906 novel by E. Nesbit), Bobbie goes down to the station and awaits the arrival of her father. This is how Nesbit describes the scene:

Bobby was left standing alone, the Station Cat watching her from under the bench with friendly golden eyes.

Of course you know already exactly what was going to happen. Bobbie was not so clever. She had the vague, confused, expectant feeling that comes to one's heart in dreams. What her heart expected I can't tell— perhaps the very thing that you and I know was going to happen—but her mind expected nothing; it was almost blank, and felt nothing but tiredness and stupidness and an empty feeling like your body has when you have been on a long walk and it is very far indeed past your proper dinner time.

Only three people got out of the 11.54. The first was a country-woman with two baskety boxes full of live chickens who stuck their russet heads out anxiously through the wicker bars; the second was Miss Peckitt, the grocer's wife's cousin, with a tin box and three brown-paper parcels; and the third—

'Oh! My Daddy, my Daddy!'

That scream went like a knife into the heart of everyone in the train, and people put their heads out of the windows to see a tall pale man with lips set in a thin close line, and a little girl clinging to him with arms and legs, while his arms went tightly around her.[33]

In the film, the suspense before the emergence of Bobbie's father is heightened by the clever use of steam from the railway engine. Bobbie stands peering down the platform. The steam has created a thick mist on which the camera (taking the perspective of the daughter) lingers. Then a tall dark shadow begins to emerge and, bit by bit, we see the gradually more visible features of the father. Then the piercing cry goes up, 'Oh! My Daddy, my Daddy!' The long-awaited homecoming has at last happened. Father and children, husband and wife, are finally reunited.

FALLING IN LOVE WITH THE FATHER

In speaking about the glorious truth of our spiritual adoption, I often use this incident as an illustration concerning the spiritual state of many believers. There are so many like Bobbie, waiting on the station, longing for their heavenly Father to emerge out of the mist, to enfold them in his arms of love. There are so many whose God is remote, and yet who long deep down to cry out, 'Oh! My daddy, my daddy!' to the one they strive to serve.

This was my own testimony for years. I was converted when I was sixteen years old, on 17 January 1977. I was privileged to be a pupil at Winchester College during a season of revival. A maths teacher called John Woolmer had prayed for a spiritual harvest at the school and was now seeing the fruit of his intercession. A large number of boys were converted between 1976 and 1977. In my own case I remember walking down Kingsgate Street late one evening and hearing a voice in my heart saying, 'If you died tonight, where would you stand before the Judgment Seat of Christ?' Up until then I had had little concern about eternity or about God, but at that moment I knew that there was terrific urgency to make a decision to repent of my sins and get right with God. So I ran round to a Christian teacher's house, knelt down on the floor, confessed my sins, received God's forgiveness, and made a decision to follow Jesus Christ to the end of my life.

For the next five years or so I was nurtured in the faith by good, solid Bible-believing friends. They taught me a simple model of prayer and how to read and study the Bible. They instilled in me the importance of going to church and attending a small group where I could be accountable for my life. They exhorted me to witness to my unbelieving friends and to walk in holiness.

On the positive side, there were lessons learnt during this phase that I never want to forget. Chief amongst these are a love of the Bible, a piety focused on Jesus, a ruthlessness over sin and a passion for souls.

On the negative side, there were lessons that I subsequently had to unlearn. These mostly had to do with legalism. There was a drivenness among us that was not healthy, and there was a definite tendency to be over-strict in certain areas. For example, I was told that I wasn't to hold a girl's hand until I was twenty-five years old and that any relationship with a girl first had to be squared with the leader of the group. All this 'heavy shepherding' led to a neurotic insecurity in my relationship with God and with others. From my perspective, God was a harsh Judge whose attitude was punitive.

The main problem with the group was this: for all its sincerity and fervour, there was too much law and not enough grace. My peers were word-centred, but they were not open to the supernatural power of the Holy Spirit. In the absence of the Spirit who brings us freedom, I was living like a slave not a son. My walk with the Lord was driven by the flesh, not led by the Spirit. Furthermore, my knowledge of God was a head-knowledge, not a heart-knowledge.

It was not until I had left this group that I began to see that this stoical form of Christianity was a warped version of genuine discipleship. At university I came into contact with charismatic Christians who were equally committed to living holy lives, and yet who had a joy and a liberty that I totally lacked. For them, the Christian life was a relationship with an intimate Father rather than a stern Judge.

Through these dear friends I began to enter into a more wholesome, functional and loving relationship with God. I had a powerful experience of the Holy Spirit in my bedroom one Christmas holiday in which my whole body shook for several minutes, and after which the Lord appeared at my bedroom door, beckoning me to follow him. I subsequently started training for the ordained ministry where I received significant healing in the area of rejection (of which more in a later chapter) and where I also had my first encounter with John Wimber's ministry. In fact, it was at a Wimber Conference in Sheffield that I experienced what I had been denied in my Christian life up until that point—intimacy in worship. As the songs were sung, I sensed the reality of God's embrace, and began to relate to him as my heavenly Father.

The biggest breakthrough came when I took my youth group to a rally in Derby in about 1987. This was a year or so after I had been ordained. I had been given responsibility for leading the young people's work at the church where I ministered. This was driving me to distraction because I couldn't get any of the young people to find any interest in being joyful, passionate Christians. My motive for taking them to the rally was to expose them to large numbers of teenagers who were enthusiastic about God and expressing that enthusiasm in heartfelt adoration.

In the event it was me rather than them that was touched and changed. I remember very vividly standing up with my youth group as the first song struck up. I remember feeling acutely self-conscious as members of my group looked around at other teenagers with their hands raised and beatific looks on their faces. I remember thinking, 'We're going to be out of here in a few minutes'. Suddenly, the band struck up a song written by Ishmael:[34]

Father God, I wonder
How I managed to exist
Without the knowledge of your parenthood
And your loving care.
But now I am your son
I am adopted in your family
And I can never be alone
'Cos Father God, you're there beside me.
  I will sing your praises,
  I will sing your praises,
  I will sing your praises,
  For evermore.

There was something not only in the melody but also in the words that moved me at first. Having been abandoned as a baby at birth, I have always been particularly sensitive about being alone. The thought of the Father being always with us was hugely encouraging and heartwarming. But what struck me most was the statement about being 'adopted' in God's family. I had never before sung a hymn or a song in which that word had appeared. As I sang out my praises to the Father for adopting me and making me his son, something was released inside me. I felt my knees turning to jelly and I sank to the ground in front of my rebellious youth group. I was in floods of tears and I couldn't do anything about it. Nor did I want to do anything about it. I knew what was happening to me was the work of the Holy Spirit and that it was about the healing of lifelong wounds.

From that moment on, God stepped out of the mist. He ceased to be a distant figure and began to be an intimate Father. In the process, I began to enter into the full certainty and joy of that spirit of adoption that I had received at my conversion. I progressed from a spirituality based on fear to one based on love. For the first time, the cry went forth from my heart to God, 'Oh! My Daddy, my Daddy!' In short, I fell in love with the Father.

THE SPIRIT OF ADOPTION

You may be tempted to feel that this is all a little sentimental. Yet on two occasions in his epistles, Paul states that God sends the Spirit of adoption into our hearts and that by this Spirit we cry out, 'Abba, Father'. Here are the two texts:

Because you are sons, God sent the Spirit of his Son into our hearts, the Spirit who calls out, 'Abba, Father'.
GALATIANS 4:6

For you did not receive a spirit that makes you a slave again to fear, but you received the Spirit of adoption. And by him we cry, 'Abba, Father'.
ROMANS 8:15

Here, then, is the conclusive proof that Christianity is not a religion but a relationship with our heavenly Father. This relationship is basically a love affair with the Trinity. Notice how all three persons of the Trinity are involved in the adoption of believers. First of all the Father chooses to adopt us into his family. He sends the Spirit of his Son, Jesus Christ, into our hearts. This same Spirit then makes it possible for us to be 'in Christ'. In other words, he enables us to enter into the intimate relationship that the Son enjoys with the Father. The primary evidence that we have entered into this Father–son relationship is that we call out 'Abba, Father' to the Living God. We address God in the same way that Jesus addressed, and indeed addresses, God. This cry comes not from our heads but from our hearts. As Jonathan Edwards constantly stressed, Christianity is therefore 'a religion of the heart'.

In Chapter 3 ('The Glorious Father') we concentrated on the Father's role in this adoptive process. In Chapter 4 ('The Son who Became a Slave'), we focused on the Son's role. In this chapter I want to explore the role of the Third Person of the Trinity in this wonderful work of adoption, for Paul makes it clear in both passages above that the Spirit of adoption is sent into the hearts of those who believe in the Son.

Now it is important right at the outset to understand that Paul is not referring to two separate experiences here. In other words, he is *not* saying the following:

First of all you believe in Jesus, then subsequently you receive the Holy Spirit by whom you are adopted into the family of God.

Paul is not indulging in a theology of subsequence. He is not saying that there is a second, subsequent blessing (after conversion) in which we receive 'the Spirit of adoption'. Rather, he is speaking about that which has made sonship possible (the work of the cross) being followed by that which makes sonship a reality (the work of the Spirit). Paul is therefore proposing the following:

Because God has done all that was necessary for our adoption through the cross, he sends into our hearts the Spirit who effects adoption.

The role of the Spirit is therefore to make the *objective* fact of our adoption a *subjective* reality in our experience.

I would say that my experience at the youth rally was a release of what I received when I first believed. In 1977 I had received the gift of the Spirit at my conversion. For years, however, I kept the Holy Spirit buried deep within the well of my heart. This was mainly due to a lack of any teaching or experience of the Spirit in those years. It was also partly due to my reluctance to face the reality of my own pain of being abandoned by my biological parents. Consequently, I had the Spirit, but the Spirit didn't have me! Ten years after my decision to follow Christ, the obstructions in the well began to be gloriously removed in a time of intimate worship. As I sang a song about my adoption by my Father in heaven, I actually felt the wellspring of divine love overflow from my heart. For the first time I could cry out, 'Abba! Daddy!' to my God. For the first time I could give my adoration to the one Tom Smail has called 'the Forgotten Father'.

THE FATHER–SON RELATIONSHIP

There is a tendency in those who have not experienced the full release of the Holy Spirit to live as slaves rather than sons. My own story is one of a person who had been adopted as a son at conversion, but who lived like a slave until much later. From Paul's point of view this is manifestly wrong. He is adamant in Romans 8:15 that we have not received a spirit that makes us a slave again to fear. Instead we have received the Holy Spirit, the Spirit of God's Son, and this Spirit evokes the 'Abba' cry from the heart of the newly adopted child. Once we become believers in Jesus, all forms of spiritual slavery must go, for we are no longer slaves but sons, and since we are sons, God has also made us heirs. *A true Christian is therefore not a person who is driven by whips but drawn by cords of love.*

This is the consistent testimony of those whom the Lord has chosen to use powerfully during seasons of revival. Thus, John Wesley really began his ministry of preaching the gospel with demonstrations of the Spirit's power *after* he had experienced the liberating power of the Spirit in his own life. It was only when his heart had been strangely warmed by God's Spirit that he exchanged the faith of a servant for the faith of a son.

This is also the testimony of Howell Harris, a contemporary of the Wesleys. He was greatly used by the Lord in the revival in Wales. Before he embarked on his preaching ministry, he had a profound experience of God. His diary records the event:

June 18th, 1735. Being in secret prayer I felt suddenly my heart melting within me like wax before a fire, with love to God my Saviour. I felt not only love and peace, but also a longing to be dissolved and to be with Christ; and there was a cry in my inmost soul, with which I was totally unacquainted before, it was this—'Abba, Father; Abba, Father'. I could not help calling God my Father: I knew that I was his child, and that he loved me; my soul being filled and satiated, crying, 'It is enough —I am satisfied; give me strength and I will follow thee through fire and water.' I could now say that I was happy indeed. There was in me 'a well of water, springing up into everlasting life', yea, the love of God was shed abroad in my heart by the Holy Ghost.[35]

Clearly, the transition from slavery to sonship can only happen through the ministry of the Spirit. This may seem something of a redundant statement to many readers, but the truth is that the vital role of the Spirit has not always been acknowledged by the great theologians of the church. Take Origen for example. Origen proposed that there were two ways of knowing God. You could either know God as Master or you could know him as Father. The first way of knowing God he called 'servitude', the second 'sonship'. He construed the differences between these two as follows:

	SERVITUDE	SONSHIP
Theology	God as Master	God as Father
Image of God	Punitive	Affectionate
Status	Slave	Son
Spirituality	Fear	Love
Understanding	Ignorance	Knowledge
Condition	Bondage	Freedom
God's Presence	Remote	Intimate

For Origen, the goal of the gospel was to bring people into a Father–son relationship with the Living God. From his point of view, this meant helping people to be delivered from a Master–servant relationship and then to progress towards that place where the 'Abba' cry could flow from their hearts. As far as Origen was concerned, those who have a Master–servant relationship know God purely and simply as God. Those who have a Father–son relationship know him as both God and Father. In the first, God is seen as the omnipotent Master who rules over us with an iron rod. In the second he is seen as the perfect Father who loves us with an incomparable passion. In the first, the believer lives in servile fear of God. In the second, he lives in filial love. In the first, the believer betrays his ignorance about the very heart of the gospel—the affirmation of the Fatherhood of God. In the second, the believer shows that he has understood the essence of the Christian faith, that we can cry out to God in the intimate language that Jesus himself used.

How did Origen propose that we move from servitude to sonship? Unfortunately, it is precisely at this point that the influence of Plato rather than the scriptures becomes visible in Origen's writings. Instead of speaking of the gracious work of the Holy Spirit in turning slaves into sons, Origen proposed a ladder of ascent. In other words, he argued that we move from slavery to sonship in progressive stages. As with all such schemes, the emphasis is very much on the believer's self-effort. It is we who have to climb the ladder and we do so as we grow in personal holiness. Thus, the purer we are, the nearer we get to the top of the ladder, where the prize of sonship awaits us. Until we get there, we have to pass through different levels in our relationship with God:

4. Son

3. Infant

2. Disciple

1. Servant

Of course, part of what Origen is saying is irrefutable. A Christian cannot expect to grow in sonship if he is not growing in holiness (2 Corinthians 6:17–18). But Origen's scheme emphasizes the human rather than the divine role in making the transition from slavery to sonship. Instead of providing a comprehensive account of the Spirit's gracious work of liberation, Origen emphasizes our role in climbing up the ladder through ever-increasing holiness. The main reason for this is because Origen himself did not have a comprehensive theology of the Holy Spirit. As Peter Widdicombe has put it, Origen's 'doctrine of the Holy Spirit is not as fully developed as his doctrine of the Son'.[36] The result is that Origen under-emphasizes the role of the Spirit in turning slaves into sons. As Widdicombe has so insightfully shown, 'the Platonic ascent has been woven into the biblical account'.[37] The resulting description of a ladder up which the believer must climb if he is to become a son is therefore flawed by a startling irony. This irony consists in the fact that Origen is unconsciously encouraging a new form of the very thing that he is trying to eradicate, namely 'slavery to law'. As Richard Lovelace has written:

Ladders are always intimidating, and it is my suspicion that Christians should always assume that they start each day at the top of the ladder in contact with God and renew this assumption whenever they appear to have slipped a rung.[38]

In the last chapter I showed how much importance Origen places on the statement of the Risen Jesus in John 20:17: 'Go to my brothers and say to them, "I am going to my Father and to your Father, my God and your God."' For Origen, this is the moment when the disciples' relationship with God changes from a Master–servant to a Father–son relationship. Now that Jesus has died on the cross and been raised immortal, the disciples no longer relate to God as slaves but as sons. They too can call God 'Father' and relate to Jesus as their Brother. In placing the emphasis on the cross and the resurrection, however, Origen has failed to stress the vital role played by the ascension of Jesus, and by the subsequent outpouring of the Holy Spirit on the Day of Pentecost. To be sure, the objective truth of our adoption as sons is sealed through Jesus' death and resurrection. But this objective truth only becomes a subjective, personal reality for the disciples once the Father's love has been poured out from heaven. Only then, when God's fire is burning within their hearts, can the disciples truly know that intimacy with the Father which constitutes the real evidence of their adoption.

As far as experience of sonship is concerned, the Day of Pentecost is therefore the defining moment. From this moment on, God has put his Spirit within us and our hearts are no longer hearts of stone but hearts of flesh (Ezekiel 36:26–27). Now the Torah is written upon our hearts (Jeremiah 31:33). The Father's desire that his people would be a kingdom of *cohanim* (literally, 'those who draw near in intimacy') is at last fulfilled (Exodus 19:6). The hearts of God's sons have truly been turned towards their Father (Malachi 4:6).

THE 'ABBA' CRY

All of this has major implications for us today. As Paul says in Romans 5:5, 'God has poured out his love into our hearts by the Holy Spirit, whom he has given us'. A burning passion for the Father has now been given to us by the Spirit. We have now entered into the Son's relationship with the Father, only we are sons and daughters by the Spirit of adoption, not by nature. As Origen rightly states, 'absolutely no one among men is from the beginning a son of God' (*Commentary on John* 20.33.290). Only Jesus is God's Son 'from the beginning'. We have sonship in a transferred not an inherent sense, as Origen showed. But we have this sonship not by struggling legalistically up the rungs of a ladder, but because the Holy Spirit has come down the ladder and lifted us up into that unending flow of love between the Son and the Father in heaven. This means that we start each day at the top of the ladder, in that place of intimate union with the Father that Jesus has made possible, and which the Spirit makes a reality in our hearts. Every day our hearts can cry out 'Abba, Father' in both private and public worship.

With that in mind, let us return to the two passages in which Paul speaks of the 'Abba' cry from the believer's heart:

Because you are sons, God sent the Spirit of his Son into our hearts, the Spirit who calls out, 'Abba, Father'.
GALATIANS 4:6

For you did not receive a spirit that makes you a slave again to fear, but you received the Spirit of adoption. And by him we cry, 'Abba, Father'.
ROMANS 8:15

Looking at these statements carefully, we reach the following conclusions:

- Believers cry out 'Abba, Father' to God. The use of the word 'cry' demonstrates that this is an exclamation of passionate and spontaneous adoration. It is not a cold, formal, liturgical statement. It is praise on fire.
- This cry is inspired by the Holy Spirit. Paul says in one context (Galatians 4:6) that the Spirit does the calling out, and in the other (Romans 8:15) that we do it by the Spirit.
- In both contexts, Paul is not only thinking of the believer's personal devotional life but the devotional life of the congregation. The 'Abba' cry is to happen in public, charismatic worship.
- In both passages, this cry is the response of the *heart* to the Spirit's work of adoption. The Spirit brings us into the Son's adoring relationship with the Father and this impacts our emotions, not just our intellects.
- It is therefore through the Spirit that we fall in love with the Father. As this happens, any slavery to fear vanishes. The perfect love given by the Spirit casts out all fear. The spirit of adoption is the opposite of the spirit of slavery.

In our theologies, we have grown accustomed to the various ministries of the Spirit. We have written about the convicting work of the Spirit, leading sinners to a place of radical repentance over sin. We have written about the vivifying work of the Spirit, leading believers into the life of the Age to Come. We have written about the revealing work of the Spirit, bringing wisdom and enlightenment to the hearts of believers. We have written about the sanctifying work of the Spirit, leading believers to ever-increasing degrees of holiness. We have written about the empowering work of the Spirit, enabling disciples to preach the gospel, heal the sick, deliver the demonized and even raise the dead. We have written about these and many other ministries. The one we have failed to look at in any depth is 'the adopting work of the Spirit'. Yet the Spirit is the Spirit of God's Son. He is the power of God's love, bringing believers into intimacy with the Living God. He is the Spirit who makes us sons and daughters of our Father in heaven. He is the one who includes us in the eternal flow of love within the Trinity, heaven's Family. How can we ever appreciate the glorious riches of God's grace without at least some consideration of the Spirit of adoption? As Jim Packer says:

If you want to judge how well a person understands Christianity, find out how much he makes of the thought of being God's child, and having God as his Father. If this is not the thought that prompts and controls his worship and prayers and his whole outlook on life, it means that he does not understand Christianity very well at all. For everything that Christ taught, everything that makes the New Testament new... is summed up in the knowledge of the Fatherhood of God. 'Father' is the Christian name for God.[39]

THE GOD OF THE BREAKTHROUGH

One of Satan's major strategies is to prevent believers from enjoying the glorious freedom of the children of God. He works tirelessly to deceive us that we have to earn the Father's acceptance through legalism. Many people become trapped by this deception, and they start to become burnt out. God seems further and further away. Christian ministry becomes an arduous duty rather than a constant joy. When this happens we become oppressed by a spirit of slavery and fear. Far from being led by the Spirit into deeper and deeper intimacy with the Father, we are driven by the flesh into greater and greater exhaustion. Instead of being drawn by cords of love into sweeter communion with Abba, Father, we are driven by whips of legalism into a lifeless, religious emptiness.

Not long ago I became acutely aware of a sense of dryness in my walk with God. In my prayer life I no longer sensed God's intimate presence. He seemed far away and remote.

One Sunday evening, after church, I talked about this with my wife, Alie. She drew my attention to a scripture, Luke 5:16: 'Jesus often withdrew to lonely places and prayed'. As we shared, I owned up to a feeling of fear concerning this verse. I confessed that I found it very hard to be alone with the Father. Whereas Alie welcomes solitude, I prefer company.

As we talked further, Alie suggested that this fear of being alone might well derive from my abandonment as a baby, and that the Lord was allowing this season of dryness in order to expose this wound in order to heal it. She also reminded me that I was due to leave for Toronto the next day in order to visit the Airport Fellowship for their annual 'Catch the Fire' conference. She urged me to pray the following prayer: 'Lord, if this is really you speaking, then send me someone at this conference whom I can really trust, who in turn will confirm this word and be used by you to bring freedom.'

Now I was keen to go to Toronto because I genuinely sensed that what was happening in that church might be the work of the Holy Spirit. So many other leaders that I knew and respected had been profoundly touched, healed and set free as a result of a visit there. In spite of my reservations about the more exotic phenomena, I had set my heart on pilgrimage and was looking forward to encountering Abba, Father afresh.

I travelled on my own and, on my arrival, sat down in my hotel room. I remember feeling utterly depressed at being so alone, and straight away phoned Alie (forgetting the time difference and waking her up in the process!) Having spoken to her, I then resorted to the television for company and comfort. Having exhausted that possibility, I finally decided to turn to God! I prayed the prayer that Alie had encouraged me to pray.

The next day I went to the first main meeting of the conference. At the end I went forward to receive prayer. The talk had not been anything to do with my own situation, but I had already decided that I was going to use every possible opportunity to get right with God and to be sorted out.

Even if the call was for infertility, I had made up my mind to go forward! After all, I could always say that I was spiritually barren.

The next hour or so changed my whole life. A woman in her fifties came towards me. She had no idea who I was, and I had no idea who she was. But she pointed her finger at my heart and said, 'Father, minister to the sense of abandonment in this man's heart.' She then looked at me and said, 'Does this mean anything to you?' I said 'Yes', and shared my story of abandonment briefly.

She then prayed for me as follows, 'Father, make up the love deficit in this man's life.' Straight away I felt this extraordinary upheaval in my stomach. I was not prone to showing emotion nor was I one to experience strong physical sensations in the presence of the Spirit. But out of my guts came this heart-rending cry of grief and anger over my abandonment. It was so powerful that I doubled up in pain and fell to the floor.

For the next few minutes I started to get in touch with an anger I had never felt before. You see, I had always been so happy with my adoptive father that I had never until that moment thought about my natural, biological father. But at that moment I realized how bitterly angry I was with him for abandoning me. I shouted out my grief and rage at him as I lay on the floor and as the woman continued to pray for me.

For what happened next you need a bit of background. About six months before this event I had been speaking at a major conference. Afterwards, a lady sent me a letter. It was expressed with great sensitivity and humility. In it she shared that she had had a vision of me while I had been speaking at the conference. She had not wanted to send it to me, but having submitted the whole matter to her pastor, she felt she had to.

In her vision she saw me speaking on a platform. I had a ball and chain around my feet and a golden key in my right hand. The lady said she had no idea what the interpretation of this revelation was, but she felt sure that I would know before long.

As I lay on the floor at the 'Catch the Fire' conference later that year, John Arnott (pastor of the Toronto Airport Fellowship) stepped up to the microphone. He said the following words: 'I see many of you with a ball and chain around your feet, especially pastors. But you have a golden key in your hands and this will unlock your chains. Forgiveness is the golden key. So forgive those who have hurt and rejected you.'

As he said those words, I knew exactly what I had to do. I shouted out, 'I forgive you, Dad. I forgive you for abandoning and rejecting me. I release you right now from my unforgiveness. May the Lord bless you, wherever you are.'

As I said this, the peace of God saturated me. I felt totally set free from the fear of rejection. I felt liberated from the slavery that had been oppressing me. In fact, I sensed a powerful deliverance going on in my life. As soon as that was complete, intimacy with God was restored. I staggered back to my hotel room a new man, no longer bound by the fear of abandonment!

THE LOVING SPIRIT OF ADOPTION

As I have reflected on the theological significance of this story—and indeed on the significance of the Toronto blessing generally—I have come back to Paul's description of the Holy Spirit as 'the Spirit of adoption'. I believe that what the British media dubbed the Toronto Blessing was in fact the Father's Blessing (as John Arnott always insisted) and that the spirit at work at the core of this movement was the loving Spirit of adoption.

In the majority of cases, the people who have been most transformed as a result of this movement have been burnt-out pastors and depressed church leaders. The stories of such men and women receiving radical inner healing are many and have been carefully documented. In my own case I am now convinced that I had become driven by the flesh, thoroughly exhausted and discouraged in my ministry. My life had become one of law rather than grace. I was striving to earn the Father's acceptance through successful ministry rather than soaking in the fire of his unconditional love.

What happened in Toronto was that the Lord exposed me to a place that was swimming in his grace. I am very aware that this place was not perfect. The over-emphasis on external manifestations by some was an error. Perhaps others might have placed more emphasis on the internal work of the Spirit bearing witness to our spirits that we are the adopted children of God (Romans 8:16). At the same time, however, I know from my own experience and the experiences of many others that God has been at work very powerfully in Toronto and that the theological category that best describes this work is 'adoption'. Thousands have fallen in love with God in that church.

The work of the Holy Spirit in our spiritual adoption is therefore absolutely critical. The Spirit continually makes real in our subjective experience the objective, finished work of the cross. To use a different metaphor, our lives are like onions. Every so often a layer of the onion needs to come off so that we can receive further healing on this journey towards wholeness in Christ. When we literally peel an onion, there are often tears. This is also the case in the spiritual aspect of our lives. As we allow the Holy Spirit to perform surgery on the next layer of our wounded hearts, so the brief pain of this results in the prayer of tears. But I have found that we are in safe hands here. We are in the everlasting embrace of the One who is the Father to the fatherless. As Abba's children, we can therefore abandon ourselves to the will of God and say 'Yes' to whatever his Holy Spirit needs to do in our lives, knowing full well that the fruit from this will be a greater understanding of the glorious freedom of the children of God. When that happens, we can truly serve Abba, Father with hearts made whole.

THE CONDITION OF OUR HEARTS

As we come to the end of this chapter on the work of the Spirit, it is important to ask what the condition of our hearts is before God. To what extent are we fulfilling the greatest commandment, 'to love the Lord your God with all your heart and with all your soul and with all your mind and with all your strength' (Mark 12:30)? If the spiritual equivalent of a heart scan was conducted on us, what would it reveal?

In Galatians 4:6 Paul says that the heart is the place from which the 'Abba' cry flows. It is the hearth in which the fire of love burns. Those who try to love God in their own strength end up with a 'hardening of the *oughteries*'. Those who go on being filled with the Holy Spirit end up with hearts on fire. Which of these describes you?

John Arnott has written, 'service is not a substitute for a love affair'.[40] At the Toronto Airport Fellowship, Arnott has consistently taught that love precedes service. All God's children are destined to serve him, but they serve him best when they are in love with him. As Arnott writes:

When the love of God impacts your heart to the fullest, no mountain is too tall, no ocean too broad, no valley too deep that you would not go through it for Him. That kind of love will cause you to serve like nothing else can. Then, rather than working for Him, you are working with Him to reach the nations of this world.[41]

So, are you in love with the Father? Have you caught the fire of love? What is the condition of your heart today?

As we continue on our journey in this book, my prayer is that the Spirit of God will deliver us from every hint of slavery, and transplant the heart of God's Son in us.

CHAPTER 6

Slavery and Sonship

We all know the story so well. A father has two sons. The younger son asks his father for his share of the estate. By making this request before his father has died, the son is indirectly saying, 'I want you dead.' In spite of the harsh and rejecting nature of the son's demand, the father gives the boy his inheritance ahead of time. The boy leaves for another country and squanders all his new wealth on loose living. After he has lost everything, he finds himself destitute and is forced to live as a farmer's slave, feeding the pigs (hardly a welcome occupation for a Jewish lad). Eventually he comes to his senses and runs home. He decides in advance how he will articulate his sorrow but finds his father already waiting for him at the gates of the village. Filled with compassion, the father runs to his son and embraces him. The boy verbalizes his repentance: 'Father, I have sinned against heaven and against you. I am no longer worthy to be called your son.' The father puts his best robe around his son's shoulders, a ring upon his finger and sandals upon his feet. A wonderful party is held in celebration of the son's homecoming.

Meanwhile, the older brother appears on the scene. He comes in from the fields where he has dutifully been slaving away all day for his father. He hears the sound of singing, dancing and merry-making. He hears from a servant that his brother has come home and that his father has killed the fatted calf in honour of the boy's return. A look of bitter resentment appears on the older son's face. He becomes angry and refuses to go into the party. So his father comes out to him and pleads with him to join in the celebration. But the son says, 'No!'

Look! All these years I have been slaving for you and never disobeyed your orders. Yet you never gave me even a young goat so I could celebrate with my friends. But when this son of yours who has squandered your property with prostitutes comes home, you kill the fatted calf for him!

The father looks sadly at his oldest son and replies:

My son, you are always with me, and everything I have is yours. But we had to celebrate and be glad, because this brother of yours was dead and is alive again; he was lost and is found.

The story finishes at this point, and it finishes in an open-ended way. There are many gaps in our knowledge of what happens next. How did the older brother react to the words of his father? Was there a reconciliation between him and his father? Did he ever celebrate the return of his younger brother? Where is the mother in the story? And so the list goes on. Yet the story concludes where it does because Jesus wants to stress that someone has been lost and yet found. In a chapter devoted to the lost (Luke 15), this is the right place to end.

THE TWO KINDS OF SLAVERY

Over the centuries there have been many different interpretations of this parable. Some have seen it as an allegory of the journey of Jesus, from Son of God to Son of Man, then from Son of Man back to Son of God. In other words, they have seen the younger son's journey to a far-off country as a picture of Jesus' descent into our sinful world. His homecoming is then viewed as a picture of his return to the Father in glory. Others have seen the parable as a picture of Israel's tragic history. The younger brother is the faithful remnant who come to a place of genuine repentance and return to their heavenly Father through the mission of Jesus. The older brother is the larger part of Israel, slaving away in the fields of law and tradition, unable to enter into the new thing that God is doing which is based on grace and unmerited love. Many and varied have been the insights into this parable during church history.

This book is about the journey from slavery to sonship. Consequently, I want to offer a new interpretation of this parable in terms of these two themes—themes that run right through the Bible, as we have already seen. From this perspective, the two sons in the story represent the two negative forms of spiritual slavery that are spoken about in the Bible. The first kind is slavery to sin, and this is represented by the younger brother. He decides to rebel against his father in the most cruel way. He goes to a far-off country and lives a life of addiction. Later on we learn this may have involved prostitution (Luke 15:30). In that place he finds himself worse off than even one of his father's hired hands. In other words, prostitution leads to destitution. He is truly enslaved.

In Romans 6, Paul talks about slavery to sin. He shows how the new believer, having been crucified and raised with Christ through baptism, has been set free from slavery to sin. A slave to sin is someone, like the younger son, who obeys the evil desires of his physical body and who offers the parts of his body to sin, as instruments of wickedness (6:13). This kind of slave has sin as his master (6:14). The apostle Peter says that such a person is a 'slave of depravity' (2 Peter 2:19). As Paul says in Romans 6:16:

Don't you know that when you offer yourselves to someone to obey him as slaves, you are slaves to the one whom you obey—whether you are slaves to sin, which leads to death, or to obedience, which leads to righteousness?

Peter says, 'a man is a slave to whatever has mastered him' (2 Peter 2:19). Once we become a new creation in Christ Jesus, however, we are no longer 'in slavery to impurity and to ever-increasing wickedness' (Romans 6:19). We are now slaves to righteousness leading to holiness. The old life of slavery, which led to spiritual death, has gone. There has been liberation and deliverance from all of that. Now believers are 'slaves to God' (6:22). They are 'noble slaves'. Having been set free from slavery to sin, out of sheer gratitude they decide to serve the Father who has rescued them.

If the younger son is a slave to sin, the older son is a slave to law. This is the second negative form of spiritual slavery. The older son has been working dutifully on his father's farm for many years. Indeed, this son says to his father that he has been 'slaving' for him and that he has never disobeyed orders (Luke 15:29). In Romans 7, Paul describes this kind of life as slavery to the law. By exposing what sin is, the law makes fascinating the very thing that it is designed to eradicate from our lives.

The sin in our lives succeeds in turning what God intended for good into something evil. For the person who is enslaved in this way, the law has become his master. Stringent and obsessive obedience to rules and regulations has become his way of life. A yoke of slavery hangs heavily upon his neck as he tries to achieve righteousness through observing the law. He is exhausted and drained by the weighty demands of self-effort. Every time he drives himself to obey his master, he finds that his flesh wars against this desire. Paul sums up this way of life in the famous words of the imaginary slave of the law in Romans 7:15–20:

I do not understand what I do. For what I want to do I do not do, but what I hate I do... I know that nothing good lives in me, that is, in my sinful nature. For I have the desire to do what is good, but I cannot carry it out. For what I do is not the good I want to do; no, the evil I do not want to do—this I keep on doing. Now if I do what I do not want to do, it is no longer I who do it, but it is sin living in me that does it.

The two sons in the story told in Luke 15 demonstrate the two forms of spiritual slavery—hedonism and legalism. The first son lives as a slave to sin in the distant country where he squanders his father's wealth. The second son lives as a slave to law in his own country as he slaves away for his father, obeying every order given to him. In a sense, both are unworthy to be called the father's sons. Yet the father chooses to address both of them as his sons, thereby wooing them towards that place where they no longer have to strive for, or against, his affections, but simply rest and rejoice in the knowledge that their father loves them. We know that the first son—the slave to sin—accepts the father's offer of compassionate love. What the second son chose to do—the slave to law—we are not permitted to know.

SLAVERY AND SONSHIP

It is easy to forget that there is a third son in Luke 15:11–32, the Son who is actually telling the story. While the two sons *in* the story model the kinds of spiritual slavery from which we need rescuing, the Son actually telling the story represents the state which we are called to receive—namely, sonship. The parable itself is an exploration of the relationship between slavery and sonship. Both boys in the story could live as sons, but both choose to live as slaves. One is restored to sonship, the other remains a slave. Meanwhile, the one telling the tale stands outside the story modelling what true sonship really entails.

If Romans 6 describes slavery to sin, and Romans 7 describes slavery to the law, Romans 8 describes the state of sonship. In Romans 8 we learn that the son is someone who knows that he is accepted by the Father. He does not live under condemnation (8:1). He is gloriously free from any slavery to the law of sin and death because the law of the Spirit of life dwells within him. The righteous requirements of the law are no longer met through strenuous self-effort, but rather through the power of the Holy Spirit. The son sets his mind on what the Spirit desires. His thoughts are therefore full of life and peace. No longer is his life controlled by his sinful nature but by the Spirit of God. No longer is he driven by the flesh, but led by the Spirit. He is no longer a slave to a fear of God's rejection and punishment. Instead, through the work of the Spirit in his heart, the son knows that the Father loves him and therefore cries out, 'Abba, Father!' As such, the Holy Spirit is constantly testifying to his spirit that he is a child of his Father in heaven and a co-heir with his Brother, Jesus Christ. He knows that God works for his good because God is a trustworthy Father. He is certain that the Father is for him rather than against him and that nothing will ever separate him from his Father's affections. In short, the son knows the Father's passion for him, and reciprocates with passion for the Father. This, then, is the essence of sonship.

During the eighteenth-century revival, John Wesley often preached about these three different states—slavery to sin, slavery to law, and sonship.[42] Using a scheme that goes back as far as Augustine, Wesley differentiated between three types of people: natural, legal and filial. The 'natural' man is what I have called a slave to sin. He is spiritually asleep and the eyes of his understanding are closed. As Wesley put it, 'clouds and darkness continually rest upon them; for he lies in the valley of the shadow of death'.[43] He is a stranger to God's law.

The 'legal' man is the person who has been shaken out of his sleep through the preaching of the gospel with the demonstration of the Holy Spirit. Wesley describes this man's spiritual condition in very vivid language:

He is terribly shaken out of his sleep and awakes to a consciousness of his danger. Perhaps, in a moment, perhaps by degrees, the eyes of his understanding are opened, and now first (the veil being in part removed) discern the real state he is in. Horrid light breaks in upon his soul; such light as may be conceived to gleam from the bottomless pit, from the lowest deep, from a lake of fire burning with brimstone. He at last sees the loving, merciful God is also 'a consuming fire'; that he is a just God and a terrible, rendering to every man according to his works... The inward, spiritual meaning of the law of God now begins to glare upon him... His heart is bare and he sees it is all sin... But though he strive with all his might, he cannot conquer... He is still in bondage and fear by reason of his sin. [44]

The 'filial' man is the one who has received the Spirit of adoption, whereby he now cries 'Abba, Father'. 'Healing light' has broken in upon the soul of the filial man. He sees the love of God in the face of Jesus Christ. He has received the pardoning love reserved for those who believe in Jesus. Consequently,

He cannot fear any longer the wrath of God; for he knows it is now turned away from him, and looks upon him no more as an angry judge, but as a loving Father. [45]

This man has received the Holy Spirit. Paul says, 'Where the Spirit of the Lord is, there is freedom! (2 Corinthians 3:17) Consequently, the filial man enjoys the glorious freedom of the children of God. He is free from the yoke of slavery to sin, and he is free from the yoke of slavery to the law. He knows that he is accepted and loved by the Father because the Spirit constantly testifies with his spirit that he is chosen, adopted and included into the Father's family. The Holy Spirit has shed abroad a passion for the Father in his heart and, as a result, his heart's cry is, 'Abba,

Father!' This is the man who has a true, living, Christian faith. This is the man who has made the journey from slavery to sonship. Hedonism and legalism hold no appeal for him. He has truly been set free.

In the table below you can see something of the differences between these three states that Wesley describes:

	NATURAL MAN	**LEGAL MAN**	**FILIAL MAN**
Spirituality	• No love or fear of God	• Fear of God	• Love for God
Insight	• Walks in darkness	• Sees things in the light of hell	• Sees things in the light of heaven
Security	• A false peace	• No peace at all	• True peace
Condition	• Licentiousness	• Bondage	• Freedom
Morality	• Sins willingly	• Sins unwillingly	• Sins not
Situation	• Neither conquers, nor fights	• Fights, but cannot conquer	• Fights and conquers!
Status	• Slave to sin	• Slave to law	• Son

Wesley's great desire was to see people enter into full sonship. He frequently preached on Romans 8:15 in the great years of revival between 1739 and 1743 (fourteen times in all). He was especially eager to help people to receive what he called 'the loving Spirit of adoption'.

Earlier, on 24 May 1738, Wesley had himself come into such a relationship with the Father. This was the year of his conversion—the year in which he exchanged the faith of a servant for the faith of a son. A change occurred in Wesley's heart as he read Luther's words about his own conversion. As Wesley recorded in his Journal (1.476):

About a quarter before nine, while he was describing the change which God works in the heart through faith in Christ, I felt my heart strangely warmed. I felt I did trust in Christ, Christ alone for salvation; and an assurance was given me that He had taken away my sins, even mine, and saved me from the law of sin and death.

This famous incident at Aldersgate Street was the turning point not just for John Wesley but also for the nation. The Holy Spirit had kindled a flame of sacred love on the mean altar of Wesley's heart. From this moment on, Wesley knew that he had been justified by faith and that he had received the Spirit of adoption by which we call God 'Abba'. His great passion was to bring others into this same saving relationship with the Father. Thousands received salvation as a result.

Wesley's passion for seeing natural and legal people progress to a filial relationship with God stemmed from his own conversion. At Aldersgate Street he made the transition from slavery to sonship. Thereafter he was determined that all within and outside the church should become sons and daughters of the Living God. As he put it: 'A few names may be found of those who love God; a few more there are that fear him. But the greater part have neither the fear of God before their eyes nor the love of God in their hearts.'[46]

One of the key themes of Wesley's preaching was therefore the full assurance of salvation. Salvation occurs as a result of believing in the finished work of the cross and receiving the Spirit of adoption. For Wesley, the inner testimony of the Spirit of adoption therefore had to accompany justification by faith. Thus Wesley could say of his own Aldersgate Street conversion:

The Spirit itself bore witness to my spirit that I was a child of God, gave me an evidence hereof, and I immediately cried, 'Abba, Father!' And this I did… before I reflected on, or was conscious of, any fruit of the Spirit. It was from this testimony that love, joy, peace, and the whole fruit of the Spirit flowed.[47]

Perhaps you can now see why I stated in Chapter 1 that it is during seasons of revival that the lost coin of adoption is rediscovered. Where the fire of God's love falls upon his church, there the 'Abba' cry goes up to heaven again.

Slavery to Sin

How does a person become a slave to sin? James gives us the answer in his letter:

When tempted, no one should say, 'God is tempting me'. For God cannot be tempted by evil, nor does he tempt anyone; but each one is tempted when, by his own evil desire, he is dragged away and enticed. Then, after desire has conceived, it gives birth to sin; and sin, when it is full-grown, gives birth to death.

James 1:13–15

James here describes a process by which a person gradually becomes enslaved by sin. At the beginning of the process, Satan tempts a person to sin. It is not God the Father who tempts us. He may permit us to be tempted, but he does not, nor cannot, tempt us himself. When Satan tempts a person, that person is presented with a choice. As the old saying goes, 'You can't stop the birds flying over your head, but you can stop them nesting in your beard.' When a person is tempted, the choice is whether or not to allow the temptation to turn into desire. If desire is allowed to form in a person's life, that will turn into sin. At this stage the person has been enticed and dragged away by the desire to sin. The subsequent life of sin that develops from this desire, if it continues, then leads in the end to spiritual death. The end of such a process is the destruction of our relationship with God, with others and with ourselves:

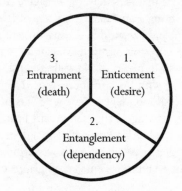

When does a person become enslaved by sin? The answer, 'when sin becomes his master'. When a person becomes powerless under the control of his addiction, then he has become totally dependent and therefore a slave. Slaves, as we saw earlier, lived under the permanent threat of death. The same is true of a spiritual slave—of a slave to sin. That person is now under the threat of spiritual death.

The apostle James says that there is a process of conception, birth and growth in the life-cycle of temptation. If we want to avoid becoming trapped in this cycle, then the best thing is not to allow the cycle to begin in the first place. A rigorous act of birth control is required. If a person does become enticed and dragged away by sin, then ruthless action needs to be taken if that person is to be set free. Radical repentance is required if the chains of such a slave are to fall off. The power of the addiction must be broken at this stage. Why? Because it will take nothing short of a miracle to bring a person who is spiritually dead through sin into a place where they are free and alive again.

Conversion is, however, such a miracle. Even the most hardened slave can be set free through the convicting, enlightening, liberating power of the Holy Spirit. The one whom Wesley called 'natural' can, through the supernatural power of the gospel, become a free man. The 'natural' man can experience what happened to the younger son in the parable of Luke 15. That son was totally entrapped by his sinful lifestyle. He was a slave to impurity and depravity and was spiritually dead in his sins. Yet even there, grace was not entirely absent from him. The father still waited and watched in the hope that his son would decide to come home. In the far-off country, the young man came to his senses. The light of revelation came into his soul and he saw that he was lost and as good as dead. He made a choice to turn from his sinful way of life. He got to his feet and resolved to say sorry to his father. He walked home, only to find that the father was standing with his arms open wide. His words of repentance were barely out of his mouth before the robe of righteousness was on his shoulders, the signet ring of affection on his finger, the sandals of the gospel of peace and reconciliation on his feet (Ephesians 6:15). Barely has he received these great gifts when a party to celebrate his homecoming is in full swing. A son who had become a slave has been restored to sonship.

He was lost, but is now found. He was spiritually dead, but is now alive. All heaven rejoices as a sinner finds freedom from slavery.

SLAVERY TO LAW

How does a person become a slave to law? When his image of God is dysfunctional and warped. When a person sees God as a hard-taskmaster or as a punitive slave-driver, he has become a slave to law. When a person does not recognize that he does not need to earn God's acceptance, that person has become a slave to law. When a person becomes Pharisaic in his attitudes—performance-oriented, hypocritical and flesh-driven—then he has become a slave to law. When a person fears a distant God, he is in a state of servitude not liberty, misery not joy, insecurity not security. In short, his spirituality is one of religion not relationship:

SLAVERY	SONSHIP
God as Master	God as Father
Law	Grace
Performance	Position
Doing	Being
External show	Internal reality
Driven by the flesh	Led by the Spirit
Fear	Love
Distance from God	Intimacy with God
Servitude	Liberty
Misery	Joy
Insecurity	Security
Religion	Relationship

This is the religion of the older brother in the parable of Luke 15. He says to his heavenly Father, 'Look! All these years I have been slaving for you.' In other words, 'All these years I have been living like a slave to law rather than as your much-loved son.' He says, 'I have never disobeyed your orders.' In other words, 'I have lived in a Master–servant rather than a Father–son relationship with you.' He says, 'You never gave me even a young goat so I could celebrate with my friends.' In other words, 'My service for you has been all misery and no joy.' He says, 'When this sinful son came home, you killed the fatted calf.' In other words, 'Your favour should be earned, not given on the basis of repentance.'

This is the bitter, Pharisaic lament of Wesley's 'legal' man. The legal man always strives to earn the Father's approval through good works. His life is dominated by the satanic lie that God only accepts those who slave away for him through strict observance of the law. Preoccupied as he is with appearances, he puts on a mask that disguises the real condition of his heart and invests much in pious, external gestures. He daily applies spiritual cosmetics in order to put on and maintain his face. His walk with God is frenetic, mechanical and lifeless. He is completely performance-driven. His identity is wholly tied up with his achievements and with the approval of others around him. He is a perfectionist and, as such, is highly judgmental of everyone else except himself. He points the finger at others and induces guilt in those he condemns. He is cold rather than warm in his relationships and relishes status and control. He is into power games and one-upmanship. He is a slave to *ought* and *must*.

The problem with this 'legal' man is that he is under deception. He is oppressed by the demonic spirit that makes a man a slave to fear (Romans 8:15). In fact, his whole life is dominated by fear:

Fear, from a lively sense of the wrath of God, and of the consequences of his wrath; of the punishment which he has justly deserved, and which he sees hanging over his head; fear of death, as being to him the gate of hell, the entrance of death eternal; fear of the devil, the executioner of the wrath and righteous vengeance of God; fear of men... (JOHN WESLEY)[48]

In essence, this fear is a fear of rejection—rejection by God (before and after death), and rejection by others. Wesley says that this fear sometimes rises to such a level in the 'legal' man that the guilty soul becomes terrified of everything, even the shaking of a leaf in the breeze. Truly, the legal man, like the older brother of the prodigal son, is a slave.

How is the 'legal' man set free? The only way is through a revelation of the Father-heart of God. That is why the father of the prodigal son reveals his heart to his oldest child. He begins with the word, 'Son' (literally, 'my child'). In these two words he reveals his desire that the older child should live in a Father–son rather than a Master–servant relationship with him. They are simple words of acceptance and affection. He continues, 'You are always with me, and everything I have is yours.' Here the father tries to get across to his son that an intimate relationship between them has always been freely available. More than that, he tries to communicate the fact that he has always had a lavish, generous attitude towards him and that his son could therefore have had absolutely anything he wanted, including a party. He continues, 'But we had to celebrate and be glad, because this brother of yours was dead and is alive again; he was lost and is found.' In this closing statement, the father reminds the boy that he is a father who loves to bring pleasure to his children, not a slave-driver who enjoys inflicting misery. 'We *had* to celebrate,' he says.

How does the older son respond? His silence is deafening at the end of the parable. While the younger brother is set free from slavery to sin, the older brother remains a slave to law. While the 'natural' condition of the prodigal son is transformed into a 'filial' state, the 'legal' state of the older brother remains the same. Both have received a stunning revelation of their father's gracious and compassionate heart. One is changed by this loving and vulnerable disclosure, the other is not. Meanwhile, the one telling the story—Jesus of Nazareth—uses this parable to unveil something of the Father's desire to turn slaves into sons. At the beginning of Luke 15, we learn that Jesus is telling this story to Pharisees and teachers of the law who are objecting to Jesus welcoming sinners. Just as Jesus chooses not to reveal the response of the legalistic brother in the story, so Luke chooses not to reveal the response of the legalistic listeners *to* the story. Both have been shown that the Father wants sons, not slaves. Both, it seems, remain in chains.

THE DEMONSTRATIVE DAD

In Chapter 3, I wrote that this parable would lose nothing and gain much if it were renamed, 'The Parable of the Perfect Father'. There is, after all, far more attention given to the character of the father than to the two sons. When Jesus introduces the parable, he does not begin by saying, 'There was a son, who had an older brother, and a father...'. But rather, 'There was a man who had two sons...'.

Right at the start of the tale, the emphasis falls not on the prodigal son, nor his jealous brother, but on the father. This is true throughout the parable. Even during the beginning part of the story, when the younger son is centre-stage (Luke 15:13–19), he is thinking out loud about his relationship with his father. Then, in the middle of the story, the spotlight falls not on the prodigal son but on the father's gracious forgiveness (15:20–24). At the end of the story, the focus is on the father's love for his hard-hearted older son (15:25–32). Indeed, the conclusion of the story (vv. 31–32) contains the words of the father not the sons. Thus the first and the last verses of the parable are to do with the father, and its beginning, middle and end revolve around his response to the two boys:

The structure of Luke 15:11–32

15:11 Introduction: The Father

15:12–19 The Beginning of the Story: The Younger Son's Rebellion Against His Father

15:20–24 The Middle of the Story: The Father's Compassion

15:25–30 The End of the Story: The Older Son's Anger Towards His Father

15:31–32 Conclusion: The Father

If a person is to make the journey from slavery to sonship, then she must be guided by the word and the Spirit into a true image of the Father in heaven. In this respect, let us remember that the Parable of the Prodigal Son is just as much the Parable of the Perfect Father, and that the father in the story is a window on to God the Father.

In Luke 15:20, a great deal of the Father-heart of God is revealed in a single verse:

But while he [the prodigal son] was still a long way off, his father saw him and was filled with compassion for him; he ran to his son, threw his arms around him, and kissed him.

What do we learn about our Father here? We learn first of all that he is a patient Father. In the New Testament, God's patience is summed up by the wonderful Greek word *makrothumia*, meaning 'long-suffering'. 2 Peter 3:9 says, 'God is patient with you, not wanting anyone to perish, but everyone to come to repentance.' In the parable in Luke 15, the father's patience with his sons is a remarkable trait. He is patient with his younger son. After his rejection at the beginning of the story, the father keeps a faithful vigil for his son at the village gates. He longs daily for the homecoming of his rebellious boy. He is truly a patient father. Unlike many human fathers, God the Father is long-suffering and forbearing.

Secondly, he is a compassionate father. While the boy was still a long way off, the father saw him and was filled with compassion for him. In Psalm 103 we learn that 'as a father has compassion on his children, so the Lord has compassion on those who fear him' (v. 13). A few verses earlier we hear that 'the Lord is compassionate and gracious, slow to anger, abounding in love' (v. 8). When the father sees his boy coming home, he is not filled with anger but pity. Unlike many human fathers, God the Father is deeply moved when he sees us wallowing in the mire of our own rebellion. His heart burns not with indignation but with compassion.

Thirdly, he is a demonstrative father. As soon as he sees his son, he cannot help but run towards him, throw his arms around him, and kiss him. This is no cold, aloof, emotionally absent father. This is a father who cannot help showing his feelings. This is a father who treasures intimacy with his children, and who loves to shower them with affection. Unlike many human fathers, therefore, God the Father lavishes his undeserved love upon us (Ephesians 1:8). As the apostle John put it: 'How great is the love the Father has lavished on us' (1 John 3:1).

Let us dwell on that last quality for a moment. I remember an occasion when my adoptive father, Philip Stibbe, shed tears over me. I had just won a scholarship to Cambridge University and the news had been given to me over the telephone. My mother and father were standing next to me, and my brother Giles was also present. When I turned to tell them the news, my father—normally restrained—couldn't help showing his feelings. With tears in his eyes, he put his arms round my shoulders and simply said, 'I'm so proud of you.' My brother Giles claims that this is one of two occasions he can recall when he saw Dad cry (the other being when Dad heard about his own father's death).

Henry Dickens tells a similar story about his father, Charles Dickens:

In the year 1869, after I had been at college about a year, I was fortunate enough to gain one of the principal scholarships at Trinity Hall, Cambridge—not a great thing, only £50 a year; but I knew that this success, slight as it was, would give him (my father) intense pleasure, so I went to meet him at Higham Station upon his arrival from London to tell him of it. As he got out of the train I told him the news. 'Capital! Capital!'—nothing more. Disappointed to find that he received the news apparently so lightly, I took my seat beside him in the pony carriage he was driving. Nothing more happened until we had got half-way to Gad's Hill, when he broke down completely. Turning towards me with tears in his eyes and giving me a warm grip of the hand, he said, 'God bless you, my boy; God bless you!'[49]

Henry Dickens wrote in 1928, 'That pressure of the hand I can feel now as distinctly as I felt it then, and it will remain as strong and real until the day of my death.'

These stories are special, but not as special as the Parable of the Perfect Father. For in both the cases above, the people concerned had done well and, as a result, could be said to have earned the demonstrative love they received. In the instance of the prodigal son, however, this is manifestly not the case. He had done nothing to deserve the father's warm and extravagant embrace. He had rebelled against his father in a very cruel and heartless way. Yet his father still ran and kissed him.

This is the kind of God that Jesus, and only Jesus, reveals. The parable of the Prodigal Son (so-called) offers us a memorable and moving glimpse of the Fatherhood of God, and it presents us with the fundamental choice of the gospel—are we going to live as slaves or as sons? The story itself involves three sons who become slaves. The younger son chooses to become a slave to sin. The older son chooses to become a slave to the law. The Son telling the story chooses to become a slave in order that we who are spiritually enslaved might become sons. As Paul put it in Galatians 4:4–5: 'But when the time had fully come, God sent his Son, born of a woman, born under law, to redeem those under law, that we might receive adoption' (NIV: 'the full rights of sons'). The third Son is the key!

A FATHER TO THE FATHERLESS

In the 1860s, Charles Spurgeon wrote the following prayer at the end of a section of teaching on spiritual adoption:[50]

O Blessed Spirit of God! Let us all now feel that we are the children of the great Father, and let our child-like love be warm today; so shall we be fit to go and proclaim the Lord's love to the prodigals who are in the distant land among the pigs.

Spurgeon makes a vital point here. He asks that believers would be so released into the loving Spirit of adoption that they become profoundly attractive to the lost. In other words, he prays that we would be so filled with the Father's love that those who do not know that love would be drawn to the Spirit at work in our spirits.

Spurgeon argued that those who have not entered into the full reality of their adoption as sons will tend to live as slaves. The spirit of slavery creeps slowly over them with the result that the Christian life becomes a hard yoke and a heavy burden. This in turn creates an unhappy church which is particularly unattractive to a lost world. As Spurgeon put it:

A body of professors [i.e. people professing to be Christians] performing religion as a task, groaning along the ways of godliness with faces full of misery, like slaves who dread the lash, can have but a small effect upon the sinners around them. They say, 'These people serve, no doubt, a hard master, and they are denying themselves this and that; why should we be like them?'

What is the alternative? The Spirit of adoption. Here is Spurgeon again:

But bring me a church made up of God's children, a company of men and women whose faces shine with their heavenly Father's smile, who are accustomed to take their cares and cast them on their Father as children should, who know they are accepted and beloved, and are perfectly content with their great Father's will; put them down in the middle of a group of ungodly people, and I will guarantee that they will begin to be jealous of their peace and joy. In this way happy saints become the most effective workers on the minds of the unsaved.

Someone once said, 'When the Father's love is restored to the Father's house, then the prodigals will come running home.'[51] The truth is that God wants his house to be a place where the fatherless feel welcome. One of my favourite verses in the Bible is Psalm 68:5: 'A father to the fatherless, a defender of widows, is God in his holy dwelling.' Throughout scripture, God reveals himself as a Father who longs to pour out his love on orphans and widows (Exodus 22:22; Jeremiah 49:11). In James 1:27, Jesus' brother says this: 'Religion that God our Father accepts as pure and faultless is this: to look after orphans and widows in their distress and to keep oneself unpolluted by the world.'

Abba, Father wants his house to be a place where the fatherless find their salvation and healing, and this applies to those who are spiritually fatherless and to those who are literally without father and mother. So let the Father's house be filled with the Father's love. Let us allow the Lord Jesus to drive out those things that prevent us from making space for the lost in our churches. Then may the prodigals come running home!

CHAPTER 7

The Cycle of Grace

Throughout this book I have mentioned how it has been during seasons of revival that the doctrine and experience of adoption has been rediscovered. This was true during the First Great Awakening in the British Isles. As we saw in the last chapter, John Wesley placed great emphasis on the Spirit of adoption in his preaching between 1739 and 1743. Throughout his entire ministry he argued that a person could not have full assurance of salvation without the inner witness of the Holy Spirit in their hearts, evoking the Abba cry.

If the lost coin of adoption was rediscovered during the First Great Awakening, it was also rediscovered during the Second Great Awakening in Charles Spurgeon's preaching. In his revival sermons during the 1860s, Spurgeon emphasized:

One work of the Holy Spirit is to create in believers the spirit of adoption... We are regenerated by the Holy Spirit, and so receive the nature of children; and that nature, which is given by him, he continually prompts, and excites, and develops, and matures; so that we receive day by day more and more of the child-like spirit. [52]

Spurgeon went on to add that this might not appear to be very important at first sight. However, he had seen enough in his ministry to know that where people are not relating to the Father as the children of God, there you will find an unhappy church. From his perspective, 'the church is never happy except as all her members walk as dear children towards God'.

A prime cause of unhappiness in the church is, for Spurgeon, a lack of emphasis upon the Spirit of adoption. When this is neglected, the spirit of slavery begins to infiltrate churches. This 'spirit of slavery' is the exact opposite of 'the Spirit of adoption'. As Spurgeon said:

Sometimes the spirit of slaves creeps over us: we begin to talk of God's service as if it were heavy and burdensome, and are discontented if we do not receive visible success. But the spirit of adoption works for love, without any hope of reward, and it is satisfied with the sweet fact of being in the Father's house, and doing the Father's will. This spirit gives peace, rest, joy, boldness, and holy familiarity with God. A man who never received the spirit of a child towards God does not know the blessing of the Christian life; he misses its flower, its savour, its excellence, and I should not wonder if the service of Christ should be weariness to him because he has never yet come to the sweet things, and does not enjoy the green pastures, wherein the Good Shepherd makes his sheep feed and lie down. [53]

These words should really be engraved on our mirrors, bedsteads and Bibles. Like Wesley, Spurgeon believed that all new converts in the revival should not only be justified by faith, but also made aware of their adoption by the Spirit of God. If they only remained aware of their justification, then there was always a danger that they would enjoy a Master–servant rather than a Father–son relationship with God. If they were taught about their adoption and encouraged to nurture a Father–son relationship, then their Christian service would not be exhausting but rather 'sweet and easy' and the church in which they served would be a happy, restful, joyful family.

Having said that, Spurgeon was no idealist. He knew from his own experience that it was unwise to be complacent in the knowledge of one's justification and adoption. Once a person has become a son or a daughter of our Father in heaven, there are still dangers. The devil's favourite strategy is to try and bewitch sons into becoming slaves again. His ploy is to oppress those who have received sonship with the spirit of slavery. Spurgeon therefore encouraged vigilance. It is all too easy, after all, for the spirit of slavery to creep slowly over us, and for service of God to become a hard rather than an easy yoke. As Paul said: 'Stand firm, then, and do not let yourselves be burdened again by a yoke of slavery' (Galatians 5:1).

THE GALATIAN HERESY

Paul gave this word of warning to the church in Galatia because this was precisely what was happening to them. They had begun their Christian lives on the right footing. Paul had come to them and preached the gospel of the cross. He had painted a picture of Christ crucified before their very eyes (Galatians 3:1). They had then chosen to believe and had received the full rights of sons (i.e. adoption). At the same time they had received the gift of the Spirit in power, resulting in miracles being worked amongst them (3:5). Furthermore, when the Holy Spirit had been poured into their hearts, their hearts had cried out, 'Abba, Father!' to God (4:6). Consequently, they were no longer slaves but sons. As Jewish believers in Jesus, the old life of stringent Torah observance had gone, and a new life of obedience based on the work of the Spirit had begun (5:16). As such, Paul could say that they were—figuratively speaking—sons and daughters of Sarah rather than Hagar (4:21–31). They were part of Isaac's line, not Ishmael's. In other words, they were sons of the free woman, not the slave woman. As Paul triumphantly announces, 'It is for freedom that Christ has set us free!' (5:1)

All this must have been great news for the new Jewish, messianic fellowship in Galatia. Yet these converts, having been gloriously liberated, were now becoming complacent. They had not yet learnt that the most common tactic of the enemy is to get adopted sons to revert to performance-oriented Christianity. By the time Paul wrote his letter to the Galatians, a group had emerged within the church that was encouraging them to go back to a punctilious and neurotic obsession with the law. These people were being manipulated by deceiving spirits into bewitching the fledgling church. The fact that Paul had to write this warning letter shows that to some extent they had succeeded.

Paul begins his letter by saying how astonished he is that the Galatian believers are so quickly abandoning a gospel based on grace for a different gospel based on law. He reminds them that the second is no gospel at all. Gospel means 'good news'. How can it be good news that we have to earn God's acceptance through legalism? The good news—especially for the Jewish people—is that we are justified by faith not by good works. As Paul writes:

We who are Jews by birth and not 'Gentile sinners' know that a man is not justified by observing the law but by faith in Jesus Christ. So we, too, have put our faith in Christ Jesus that we may be justified by faith in Christ and not by observing the law, because by observing the law no-one will be justified.
GALATIANS 2:15–16

It is through Jesus, then, that a person is set free from their slavery to the law. It is particularly through the cross and the Spirit that true liberty comes to those under the law.

Through his death on the cross, Jesus delivers us from the curse of the law. The finished work of the cross has achieved all that is necessary for us to be declared and made righteous in the sight of God. Through the cross, we have been delivered from slavery into sonship. As in the old Roman rite of adoption, we have been bought out from the slave-driving influence of our original father (the devil) and placed under the loving affection of our new Father in heaven. This act of redemption and emancipation has been purchased not through gold or silver but through the precious blood of Jesus Christ—the Son who became a slave. Through the power of the cross, we have been made sons and daughters of our Father in heaven. We have been delivered from the curse of legalism and liberated from the spirit of slavery. Now we have a new father, a new family, a new home and a new name.

Through the cross, then, Jesus sets us free from the prison house of legalism (Galatians 3:23). But Jesus not only died on the cross, he rose again, ascended into the heavens, and poured out the Holy Spirit on the Day of Pentecost. This means that receiving the Spirit is necessary as well as believing in the finished work of the cross. Adoption is important as well as justification. Through faith in Jesus we become sons and daughters of God (Galatians 3:26). That's the believing part, if you will. But because we are sons and daughters, God sends the Spirit of adoption into our hearts. That's the receiving part. The Holy Spirit brings us into the subjective realization of what has been objectively achieved on the cross—namely, a filial, intimate, heartfelt relationship with God the Father. Through the work of the Spirit, we become aware that we are the chosen, adopted children of God. We enter into that same relationship which the Son enjoys with the Father. Like him, we cry 'Abba, Father' as we pray to God. Thus Paul says to the Galatians that they should no longer be driven by the flesh but led by the Holy Spirit. The former 'walk', based as it was on *halakah* (moral rules) is now replaced by the call to keep in step with the Spirit. This is the way of sons rather than slaves.

THE CYCLE OF GRACE

The bad news is this: the Galatian heresy is alive and well in the church of Jesus Christ today. There are many Christians preaching justification by faith but living a life of justification by business. There are many genuinely 'born again' people who have been deceived by Satan into believing that they have to earn God's acceptance through exhausting labours and visible successes. Consequently, even in Bible-believing contexts, many churches are promoting a frantic and restless worka-holism that is no antidote at all to a busy and noisy world. They are what Charles Spurgeon would have called 'unhappy churches', full of people who have fallen foul of the neurotic attempt to gain acceptance through achievement. This, according to the late Frank Lake, is the source of depression.

In Frank Lake's magisterial book, *Clinical Theology*, there are several pages on which the author provides a lasting defence against this tempt-ation to revert to performance-driven Christianity.[54] On these pages, Lake describes what he calls the dynamic Cycle of Well-Being. This cycle represents the spirit of life in Jesus Christ and it sets a person free from slavery to the law. Lake argues that this cycle—which we might call 'the Cycle of Grace'—is the answer to the depression that is prevalent in so many churches. If those who have become depressed can learn to flow in the cycle of Jesus' well-being, then they will not only receive healing themselves, they will also function as a conduit of the well-being of Jesus to others who are depressed. Put in less clinical, more Spurgeon-like language, an unhappy church will become a happy church, which in turn will become profoundly attractive to unhappy people.

Let us look at the Cycle of Grace:

1. Acceptance. Lake's thesis is that all believers need to begin with the knowledge that they are accepted by the Father. This acceptance is freely given by the Father through the Son and by the Holy Spirit. We can approach the Father's throne with confidence because we have been justified by faith in Christ, baptized (the 'sign of God's *acceptance* of us') and adopted into the fellowship of the church.

2. Sustenance. As we go on being filled with the Spirit of God and growing in holiness, this sense of acceptance by the Father increases in our hearts. As we progress in sanctification, as we commune with the Lord through the Eucharist, as we continue to grow in grace, the knowledge that the Father accepts us in his Beloved Son sustains us in both the joys and sorrows of the Christian life. As this happens, the God of all hope fills us with all joy and peace in believing.

3. Significance. (Lake actually uses the word 'status', but this has become such a loaded term in our culture that I prefer 'significance'.) Our significance derives not from what we do but from who we are. As the Spirit testifies to our spirits that we are children of God, the sense of the Father's heredity within us conquers the need to strive. The search for significance is therefore ended with the Spirit-given revelation of our position, or status, as sons and daughters of God.

4. Achievement. Having come to a sure understanding that we are accepted, we are not only sustained and built up by that knowledge, we are also motivated to bear fruit as Christians. Instead of doing good works in order to earn the Father's approval, we do good works because we already know that he approves of us. We have a destiny that needs to be seized and a work that only we can do. We fulfil our destiny by being led by the Spirit, not driven by the flesh.

The well-being of Jesus

Frank Lake rightly says that this Cycle of Grace is visible in the life of Jesus and, indeed, that it was the source of his well-being. If we look at Mark's account of Jesus' baptism in the River Jordan, we can see how true this is:

At that time Jesus came from Nazareth in Galilee and was baptized by John in the Jordan. As Jesus was coming up out of the water, he saw heaven being torn open and the Spirit descending on him like a dove. And a voice came from heaven: 'You are my Son, whom I love; with you I am well pleased.'

MARK 1:9–11

1. Acceptance. Before Jesus begins his kingdom ministry, he receives a revelation of the Father's special love for him. This revelation occurs as the Spirit falls upon him like a dove. This is not an anointing for sonship, as the Adoptionist heretics proposed, but an affirmation of an already existing sonship. Over Jesus, the Father declares his special love. From now on, the Son will minister from the firm foundation of the Father's acceptance.

2. Sustenance. Throughout Jesus' ministry, this sense of the Father's acceptance sustains him. Jesus knows that the Father loves him for who he is not what he does. Jesus addresses God as 'Abba'—the language of intimacy. At the critical moments of his ministry (such as the transfiguration), Jesus receives a fresh disclosure of the Father's special affection for him. On the Mount of Transfiguration, the Father declares: 'This is my Son, whom I love. Listen to him' (Mark 9:7).

3. Significance. The Son's sense of self-worth is wholly tied up with the value placed on him by his heavenly Father. His identity is not associated with what he does, but rather with who he is. As a result, we see in Jesus a person who is happy to be himself. We see a person who is truly free to be. The surest sign of this is Jesus' use of 'I am' in his teaching. Jesus rests in the knowledge of how the Father sees him:

I am the Bread of Life (John 6)
I am the Light of the World (John 8)
I am the Gate (John 10)
I am the Good Shepherd (John 10)
I am the Resurrection and the Life (John 11)
I am the Way, the Truth and the Life (John 14)
I am the True Vine (John 15)

4. Achievement. Jesus is conscious that he has been given a unique work to do. In John 5:36, he speaks about the task he has been given by the Father to complete. This task is to die on the cross and to take away the sin of the world. At Calvary, he cries, 'It is finished.' This is a cry of success, not defeat. Jesus says, 'I've done it! I've succeeded! I've achieved all that I was destined to.' He has done this all on the basis of his acceptance by the Father.

LIVING AS SONS AND DAUGHTERS OF GOD

Anyone who wants to live as an adopted child of God needs to live in this same cycle of grace and well-being. In other words, if we want to live as sons, we must live like the Son. This means serving God with hearts made whole. How are our hearts made whole? Through the Spirit-given revelation that the Father himself accepts us, and through the knowledge that we are children not through our achievements, but by his adopting grace.

For this to happen, we must help believers to start their Christian lives on the right footing. As Lake has spotted, this has implications for our whole approach to Christian initiation. The Christian life needs to start with the certain knowledge of our *acceptance* by God through the grace of justification and adoption. This inward grace needs to be expressed outwardly through baptism. Baptism is a rite in which the adopted son says to the church and to the world, 'I am *in* Christ and therefore an adopted son/daughter of my heavenly Father.' It is an outward sign of the inward reality of adoption into sonship—a truth much better understood by the early church Fathers than it is by us today. John Chrysostom wrote this about the newly baptized: 'You who were a slave, a captive and a rebel have suddenly been raised to adoption as a son' (*Baptismal Homilies* 5.22). In an earlier section (3.5) he waxes lyrical about the change in status enjoyed by the baptized believer:

You... are now free and citizens of the Church; you who were lately in the shame of your sins, are now in freedom and justice. You are not only free, but also holy; not only holy, but also just; not only just, but also sons; not only sons, but also heirs; not only heirs, but brothers of Christ!

Clearly the church Fathers had a far keener understanding than we do that baptism is the outward sign of an inner liberation from slavery into sonship (through adoption).

At baptism, the new believer chooses to identify with the death and resurrection of the Son of God. Going beneath the waters, he dies with Christ. Emerging from the waters, he rises with Christ. In the process, he dies to the old way of life and to his old identity. He hears the voice of the Father declaring that he too is a beloved son, in whom the Father is well pleased. Now he enjoys the legal status of a child of God.

As such, baptism is not unlike the old Roman rite of adoption. In the act of immersion, the new believer comes out from under the *patria potestas* of Satan and is subsequently placed under the *patria potestas* of the Living God. Through baptism, the believer loses his old identity and acquires a brand new identity, a new family name, and a new inheritance. In short, he becomes a brand new creature in Christ Jesus.

When I was adopted as a baby, I lost my old name and my old family. I have no idea who my natural father was. On my birth certificate, the word 'unknown' is written where my father's name should be. At my adoption, I acquired a brand new surname and entered a brand new family. To all intents and purposes, my old identity was erased and I started a completely new way of life. When the judge handed my new birth certificate to Philip and Joy Stibbe, he declared me adopted and made me legally a son and heir of the Stibbe household. From that time on, my identity was tied up with the Stibbe name, the Stibbe family tree, and the Stibbe way of life.

Our acceptance by the Father is therefore the foundation of our Christian lives. Before we *do* anything for God, we know that we *are* beloved by God. By grace, we have brand new identities as sons and daughters, and we are brand new creatures. Being loved by the Father becomes the very core of our existence. This is both our legal and actual status before God.

From this time on, our sense of acceptance needs to be *sustained* in the right way or we will go back to the old life of striving to earn God's acceptance through our achievements. Whatever words were spoken over our lives by previous father figures, our heavenly Father's word is one of affirmation and affection. He does not say, 'You're worthless', or, 'You'll never be any good'. Rather, he says, 'You are my beloved son or daughter; I'm very pleased with you.' Whenever Satan tries to bring us into a place of inferiority, condemnation and low self-esteem, we therefore reply, 'I am Abba's child.' We resist the enemy's constant attempts to draw us into a place of self-rejection by reaffirming what the word of God says (that we have been predestined for adoption as sons) and by hearing what the Holy Spirit says to our own spirits (that we are the children of God). In short, we remember our baptism!

From now on, our sense of *significance* derives not from our performance but our position in Christ. Who we are, and indeed *what* we are, derives from the fact that we are adopted by grace. From this knowledge flows our sense of value. No longer are we preoccupied with the way others see us. We are wholly taken up with the way the Father sees us. No longer are we seeking the approval of others, we seek a deeper revelation of the Father's exquisite perspective of us. When the devil tries to exasperate us with what was true about the old self, we respond by reasserting the truth about our new self:

I have been given the right to be a child of God (John 1:12).
I am no longer a slave but a friend of Christ (John 15:15).

I have been bought for adoption through Christ's blood
(1 Corinthians 6:20).
I was predestined for adoption (Ephesians 1:5).
I am a child of Abba by adoption (Romans 8:15).
I am God's work of art (Ephesians 2:10).
I am no longer under any condemnation (Romans 8:1).
I cannot be separated from the Father's love (Romans 8:35).
I am loved by the Father himself (John 16:27).
I have been redeemed and forgiven (Colossians 1:14).
I am a citizen of heaven (Philippians 3:20).
I have not been given a spirit of fear (2 Timothy 1:7).
I am no longer a slave but a son (Galatians 4:7).
I am seated with the Son in heaven (Ephesians 2:6).
I am of the same family as Jesus (Hebrews 2:11).
I am a brother of the Lord Jesus (Hebrews 2:11).
I can approach the Father with confidence (Hebrews 4:16).
I am a brand new person in Christ Jesus (2 Corinthians 5:17).

If our sense of significance derives from sonship not slavery, then we will be able to achieve God's purpose for our lives. The reason for this is because we will be ministering for the Lord out of a sense of gratitude rather than a need for God's approval. This, if you think about it, is the proper response of a liberated slave. The slave who has been delivered from his chains through the generosity of another will want to express his gratitude by serving his emancipator. A helpful illustration of this is the incident that occurred in the USA in the days before slavery was abolished.

Abraham Lincoln, it is said, bought a slave-girl with the sole intention of setting her free. She had no idea that this was what he was doing. She believed that this was a normal sale and that she was about to begin a life of service under a new master. However, once Lincoln had paid the price for her, he gave her the legal documents that told her that she was now free. At first she couldn't understand what was going on. Lincoln had to keep repeating to her, 'You're free!' 'You're free!' As the full realization of what had happened began to sink in, she asked Lincoln, 'Am I free to go wherever I want and do whatever I want to do?' He replied, 'Indeed you can'. 'Then,' she said, 'I choose to stay with you and to serve you gladly for the rest of my days.'

The fact is, God the Father has set us free from slavery and, through the blood of his Son, given us the status of adopted sons and daughters. This is indeed good news! The right response is to transfer our loyalty and service from our former master (the father of lies) to our new, adopting Father (the King of Kings). We are no longer driven like slaves in order to earn God's acceptance. We now realize that our redemption from slavery is irrefutable and undying testimony to our acceptance. Now we gladly choose to live as the noble slaves of Almighty God, whose service is perfect freedom.[55] We serve him with our whole hearts because we are moved to do so by the limitless depths of his love. In this way, our achievements flow out of our acceptance.

THE QUESTION OF IDENTITY

There was once a bishop who came to the time of his retirement. Those who worked with him decided that it was now time to have his portrait painted so that his picture could hang with those of all the previous bishops in that diocese.

A modern artist was commissioned to paint the portrait and, over a number of sittings, the picture began to take shape. When the great day of the unveiling arrived, however, the assembled dignitaries gasped in horror as the painting was uncovered. For there, on the canvas, was a ghastly demonstration of meaningless, abstract art. Most of the picture contained extravagant colours and jumbled mathematical shapes. In the middle, barely visible, was the rough outline of a person's face.

The bishop was asked what he thought of the painting. Without a moment's hesitation he replied, 'Matthew 14:27: "Take heart, be not afraid, it is I!"'

While we rely on the way others see us, our sense of identity is always going to be confused. We will build our sense of who we are on what we do, and on what other people think of what we do. Since few people are given an exclusively positive portrait of their personalities and achievements, this is indeed dangerous ground. We will not be happy with our identities and we will tend to suffer, deep down, from negative self-esteem. The chances are we will be like Gonzo, that misshapen and anarchic character in *The Muppet Show*, who once sang the following words on a TV programme I watched:

> *I wish I had a coat of silk*
> *The colours of the sky;*
> *I wish I had a lady fair*
> *As any butterfly;*
> *I wish I had a house of stone*
> *That looked upon the sea;*
> *But most of all I wish that I*
> *Was someone else but me.*

Believers who live in the Cycle of Grace will not have a negative sense of self-worth. Their identity will be based on who they are and what they are in Christ Jesus. It will not be based on what they do for the Lord, nor on the compliments of others. The identity of the adopted child of God is derived from the Father's loving declaration that he is a beloved son who brings pleasure to God's heart. This, if you will, is the *true self*. It is human identity as it was designed and destined to be. The *false self*, on the other hand, is a demonic distortion of human identity. It is identity based on work and approval. This means that while the false self derives identity from personal achievements and the adulation of others, the true self derives its identity from being forgiven and loved by God.

The sad truth is that even within the church there are people who are operating out of the false self. Such people usually suffer from work or approval addiction. The work addict is someone who builds their identity on what they do. The approval addict is someone who builds their identity on the plaudits of others. In the following table you will see how all this hangs together. In the first column you will see these two kinds of addiction. In the second column, the symptoms associated with this addiction. In the third, the consequences:

ADDICTION	SYMPTOMS	CONSEQUENCES
• Work	• Identity tied up with ministry and with excessive labour	• False self, burn-out, striving
• Approval	• Identity tied up with how others see me and with compliments	• False self, insecurity, striving

In both cases, the believer has been duped by the spirit of slavery and has lost a sense of their God-given sonship. As a consequence, the believer has started to go the opposite way round the Cycle of Well-Being. He is beginning with achievements, then proceeding to significance, then to sustenance, in the forlorn hope that all this will create a sense of acceptance. In other words, he has turned the Cycle of Grace into a Cycle of Law:

The work and approval addicts therefore begin by striving to achieve through laborious ministry and through the positive views of fellow Christians. Having started on this road, they believe that their temporary successes will sustain their need to succeed, to be loved, and to be someone special. This, in turn, results in a false sense of personal worth, significance and identity. The end they long for is to be accepted by God, by others, and by themselves. Sadly, this is never what they actually receive.

Living in the Cycle of Law can never provide a believer with any lasting happiness. Like every addiction, there is a temporary feeling of euphoria followed by a deep sense of unfulfilled desire. Pleasure is so quickly followed by pain. The only way back on track is for the believer to recognize that his true self is founded on the two truths mentioned in Chapter 1: justification and adoption. The work addict needs to remember that she is justified by faith through grace, not by her good works or tireless ministry. The approval addict needs to remember that she is adopted by God's grace, and that she already has the approval of the Father. In other words, the believer trapped in the Cycle of Law needs to go back to basics and recognize that her acceptance by the Father is based on her justification and adoption, not on her works or successes. Thus, the God-given cure for work and approval addiction is justification and adoption. Applied by the Spirit, the revelation of these two glorious doctrines will deliver an oppressed believer from slavery into sonship:

DISEASE	CURE	HEALING	RESULT
• Work addiction	• Justification by simply believing in Jesus	• Grace	• Identity tied up with being 'just as if I'd never sinned'
• Approval addiction	• Adoption by the work of the Holy Spirit	• Grace	• Identity tied up with being accepted as Abba's child

The believer who lives in the reality of her justification and adoption will travel the right way round the Cycle of Grace. She will know that she is right with the Father and that she is loved by the Father. As such, she will be better equipped to resist the devil's attempts to nurture a false self, and she will find greater freedom in cultivating the true self of the child of God.

THE TRUE BASIS OF ASSURANCE

Returning to Mark 1:9–11, we learn something vital about our assurance of the Father's acceptance from the story of Jesus' baptism. In Mark 1:10, we see the heavens torn open and the Holy Spirit descending on Jesus like a dove. The next moment we hear the Father's words, spoken through the torn heavens: 'You are my Son, whom I love; with you I am well pleased.' First comes the anointing of the Spirit. Second comes the revelation of God's word. In the final pages of this chapter, we will see that it is both the Spirit and the word which provide us with the full assurance of sonship. While Jesus' baptism cannot be an exact model for us, it does highlight the two main ways in which the Father reveals his acceptance of us.

Let us look first of all at the role of the Spirit. As Jesus comes up from the waters, the Spirit comes down from the heavens. From this point on, the Holy Spirit remains upon Jesus and he can say, in his inaugural sermon, 'The Spirit of the Sovereign Lord is upon me' (quoting Isaiah 61:1). Jesus is now seen as the Servant in Isaiah 40—55, about whom Yahweh says:

> Here is my servant, whom I uphold,
>   my chosen one in whom I delight;
> I will put my Spirit on him
>   and he will bring justice to the nations.
>
> Isaiah 42:1

If Jesus had any doubts about his unique sonship prior to his baptism, he certainly has none afterwards. The Holy Spirit has descended upon him and now testifies with his spirit that God is his Father and that he is the Son of God from eternity to eternity. Even the devil doesn't question this unique, filial status. In the very next episode after the baptism, Jesus' temptation in the wilderness, he does not say, 'If you are the Son of God'. He says, 'Since you are the Son of God'. The devil knows that Jesus is divine.

What is true for Jesus is true for us. It is the Holy Spirit who affirms that we are the sons and daughters of God. There is a major difference, of course. We become the sons and daughters of God by adoption, while Jesus is the Son of God from eternity. This means that in our case the Spirit affirms the fact that we have been adopted as the children of God. In Jesus' case, the Spirit affirms the fact that he is already the Son of God. For Jesus, Sonship is a case of being. For us it is a case of becoming. In our case, the Spirit testifies with our spirits that we are the adopted children of God.

One of the questionable aspects in the charismatic renewal has been the tendency to trust in external sensations rather than inward communion as the basis of assurance. There has been an unspoken tendency to thirst after bodily reactions to God's power more than the inner testimony of the Spirit. This has created a culture in which shaking, falling, laughing, weeping, jerking and groaning have become the only signs that God truly loves and accepts us. Those who experience these things feel affirmed by God's touch. Those who don't experience them feel rejected and left out.

Jonathan Edwards wrote a great deal about the dangers of this particular tendency back in the First Great Awakening in eighteenth-century America. By the time he wrote his classic work, *Religious Affections*, he had become very cautious about the more sensational phenomena associated with revival. For Edwards, the true sign of grace in a believer's life was not constant visions (much of which he attributed to the imagination), nor the 'bodily exercises' (such as shaking and falling), but those operations on the heart that are spiritual, supernatural and divine. In other words, Edwards looked on the heart of a person rather than on his outward appearances. His chief concern was whether or not a person knew in his heart something that could never have been discovered naturally and could only have been communicated through the work of the Holy Spirit. Did a person know the royal seal of the Prince of Princes? Did he know that the seal of the High King of heaven had been stamped upon his heart? This was what Edwards meant by the 'divine' operation of the Spirit, for nothing could be more divine than the revelation that we are God's children.

This, then, is what Edwards called the *witness* of the Spirit—the revelation that we are the adopted children of God with attendant evidence of that fact in our lives. For Edwards, the crucial passage of scripture in this whole area is Romans 8:16, where Paul says that the Spirit witnesses to our spirits that we are the children of God. Edwards showed that the Spirit referred to is the Spirit of adoption that dwells in us, leads and guides us, and disposes us to behave towards God as children towards a father. This is the Spirit of love that creates 'the disposition and temper of children, appearing in sweet childlike love to God, which casts out fear or a spirit of a slave'.[56] Once the believer knows this internal work of the Spirit, he will never need 'multiplied signs' because he feels plainly the intuitive and immediate union with Abba, Father. This kind of operation could never be created by the flesh or inspired by the devil. While both an unholy and the human spirit can suggest scriptures and give false visions, neither can lead to genuine intimacy with Abba, Father.

It is therefore the Holy Spirit who confirms that we are accepted and loved by Abba, Father. But the word of God also plays a part. In the account of Jesus' baptism, a voice is heard from heaven crying, 'You are my Son, whom I love; with you I am well pleased' (Mark 1:11). It is supremely important to understand that when the Father speaks, he speaks using the language of the Hebrew Bible. 'You are my Son' occurs in Psalm 2:7. The rest occurs in Isaiah 42:1. The Father's acceptance of his Son is therefore communicated by the word as well as the Spirit. What is true for Jesus is also true for us. Our adoption is affirmed through the inner testimony of the Spirit and the written testimony of the word of God.

It is interesting to draw a parallel once again with my own adoption. The evidence of my adopted sonship is twofold: First of all, there is the potent testimony of my own experience of being accepted, nurtured and loved by my adoptive parents; that is the evidence of my heart. But there is also the external evidence of the legal adoption papers signed way back in 1960. That is the evidence provided by the courts of this land. In truth, I need both.

In the case of our spiritual adoption, God gives us the same twofold evidence that we are the beloved children of God. There is first of all the inner testimony of the Spirit. This impacts the spiritual part of our humanity with the revelation that we are sons and daughters, and draws out the 'Abba' cry from our grateful hearts. But there is secondly the evidence of the word of God which functions like a legal document, telling us as a matter of fact that we are adopted by Abba Father, through his Son Jesus Christ, in the power of the Holy Spirit. The Spirit and the word therefore form the sure foundation of acceptance by the Living God. In truth we need both.

Someone has said that it is much easier to fall in the Spirit than it is to walk in the Spirit. This may well be true. It is easier to respond outwardly to the power of God than to go on opening one's inner life to the transforming power of the loving Spirit of adoption. We need to encourage one another to say the following daily:

God's word tells me that I'm an adopted child of God and that I'm infinitely loved. Holy Spirit, I welcome you into my life afresh today. Please bring a new revelation to my spirit that Abba, Father loves me for who I am and not for what I do. Please place me once again under the affirming radiance of the Father's smile.

As you read this, may the Lord bless you and keep you; the Lord make his face shine upon you and be gracious unto you; the Lord turn his face towards you and give you peace.

CHAPTER 8

Keys to Glorious Freedom

In the Second World War, my father Philip Stibbe was captured and made a prisoner of war for over two years. He suffered terribly during that time but managed to survive and was eventually released. On his return to England, he wrote a book about his experiences called *Return Via Rangoon*. The final section of the book, entitled 'Deliverance', describes the unforgettable moment when and he and his column of POWs heard that they were now free:

There was a sudden unearthly silence and, speaking in a strained but clear voice so that everyone could hear, the Brigadier said, 'At last I can tell you something that you have been waiting to hear for years; we are all free men.' There was an audible gasp of astonishment and a few seconds passed while this amazing news sank in; then there was a shout of joy as the full realization of what it meant came over us. We all went completely crazy, patting one another on the back, shaking hands, laughing and weeping simultaneously.

We were free. The strain under which we had lived for so long was suddenly lifted and the feeling of relief was almost unbearable. Now for the first time for years we could look forward confidently to the future we had almost despaired of at times, to our homes and families, to a civilized life instead of a bare existence. For years all this had seemed a dream so utterly desirable that we hardly dared to imagine that it could ever come true and, now that it had happened, we were almost too dazed to realize it. [57]

This book has been a celebration of our spiritual adoption. It has also been an exploration of the freedom that we have in Christ. Through our adoption we have been given something almost too good to be true. We have been granted a new freedom, a new family, and a new future. Like slaves in ancient Rome, or POWs in the Second World War, we have been liberated from oppression and given a glorious liberty (Romans 8:21).

In this final chapter I want to describe some of the major keys for enjoying the glorious freedom that comes from our spiritual adoption. These keys are not steps in some systematic 'How to' programme. They are part of a complex of the Spirit's work of liberation and healing. In these remaining pages I want to show in practical terms how we can unlock the chains that inhibit us from experiencing the freedom given by the loving Spirit of adoption. If you are anything like me, then the Lord will not unlock all of these chains at one time. He will deal with the right issues in the right way at the right time. Here, as in everything else, we need to let God be God. Put another way, Father knows best.

KEY 1: DEALING WITH DECEPTION

One of the main reasons why believers don't enter into the full liberty of their spiritual adoption is because of faulty theology. Throughout this book we have seen how God wants us to make the journey from slavery into sonship. In Paul's theology the experience of the Holy Spirit is crucial here. To be sure, we cannot go from slavery to sonship without Jesus Christ. As I have constantly shown, it is Jesus who has opened up the way by which slaves become sons. But Paul also says that it is the Holy Spirit who applies the benefits of the finished work of Christ to our lives. It is the fire of God that causes our hearts to acknowledge our adopted sonship and to cry out 'Abba, Father'. Without the empowering presence of the Holy Spirit, we cannot actually experience the glorious freedom of the children of God. We may know our freedom as an intellectual fact, but we will not know it as a heartfelt reality. There is therefore an unavoidable, charismatic dimension to our adoption.

During church history there has often been a neglect of the experience of the Holy Spirit. Frankly, it is amazing how quickly Paul's emphasis on 'demonstrations of the Spirit's power' fades from view. The journey from slavery to sonship remains a popular theme in the early church, to be sure. This is especially true in the Alexandrian tradition; Origen and Athanasius are very keen on it.[58] But the means of getting from slavery to sonship undergoes a subtle change in the post-apostolic church. No longer is it the invasion of the fire of love that constitutes the key factor in the process. Now it is strenuous self-effort that gets a person from servile fear to filial love.

In the second-century Christian text entitled *The Shepherd of Hermas* (c. AD140), the author tells a story in which a slave becomes a son. This parable reveals the continuing popularity of the slave–son contrast in the first centuries of the church. It also highlights how spiritual discipline quickly replaces charismatic experience as the vital factor in turning slaves into sons:

A certain man had an estate and many slaves. He turned a portion of his estate into a vineyard; and chose a certain slave who was trusty, well-pleasing and held in honour. He called him and said, 'Take this vineyard I have planted, and put a fence around it until I return. Do nothing else to it. Now keep this commandment, and you shall be free in my house.' Then the master of the servant went away to travel abroad.

When he had left, the servant put up a fence around the vineyard; and having finished the fencing he noticed that the vineyard was full of weeds. So he reasoned to himself, saying, 'This command of my lord I have carried out. So I will now weed this vineyard. Then it will be tidier. Without the weeds it will yield more fruit.' So he tilled the vineyard, and uprooted all the weeds that were in the vineyard. This vineyard subsequently became very orderly and fruitful, because it had no weeds to choke it.

After a time the master of the estate returned, and he went into the vineyard. Seeing the vineyard fenced neatly, and cultivated as well, with the weeds uprooted and the vines flourishing, he rejoiced at what his servant had done. So he called his beloved son, who was his heir, and the friends who were his advisers, and told them what he had commanded his servant, and how much he had found done. And they rejoiced with the servant at the testimony which his master gave.

And he said to them, 'I promised this servant his freedom, if he should keep the commandment which I gave him; but he not only did what I asked but did a good work on top of that, and this has pleased me greatly. Therefore, for this work which he has done, I want to make him joint-heir with my son, because, when the good thought struck him, he did not neglect it, but fulfilled it.' And the son of the master gladly agreed that the servant should be made joint-heir with the son.

After some few days, his master made a feast, and sent the servant many delicacies from his table. But when the servant received them, he took what was sufficient for himself, and then distributed the rest to his fellow-servants. And his fellow-servants, when they received this choice food, rejoiced, and began to pray for him, that he might find greater favour with the master, because he had treated them so handsomely.

The master heard about all these things, and again rejoiced greatly at his servant's behaviour. Once again he called together his friends and his son, and announced what the servant had done with his delicacies. Consequently, they became even more enthusiastic about the master's resolve to make his servant joint-heir with his son.

In its original context, this parable is concerned with fasting. The Shepherd tells the story of a person who was called to go one mile, but willingly went two instead. The moral is clear. If you embark on a spiritual discipline, make sure you do more than the minimum required. That way you will please God and earn his favour and, as a reward, he will turn you from being a slave into a son.

Now undoubtedly there is an element of truth in this. If one is going to give, fast, pray, whatever, then this needs to involve self-sacrifice if it is going to be meaningful. Unfortunately, however, the parable also gives the strongest indication that the journey from slavery to sonship is made through strict observance of religious duties rather than by receiving the loving Spirit of adoption. Indeed, the very image used of God here—Master—underlines this, as does the notion that his favour is earned rather than given. The message is therefore clear: We gain our freedom through obeying regulations about fasting rather than through receiving the Spirit of adoption. Slaves become sons by fasting twice as rigorously as God requires.

It is this view which constitutes one of the great deceptions of the church. Paul spoke about the 'bewitching' power of this legalistic aberration. By using the word 'bewitch' he revealed its satanic origin. Paul knew that the enemy is constantly trying to get those who preach justification by faith to live the opposite (justification by works). Paul understood that this was a demonic lie and that it needed to be exorcized from the church. If we are to enjoy the glorious freedom of the children of God, then we too must rid ourselves of any hint of this deception. We have to acknowledge that we become the adopted children of God by believing in Jesus Christ and by receiving the flame of divine love. For this to happen we must be open to genuine, charismatic experience, for it is the Spirit of God who brings us into the Son's relationship of holy intimacy with Abba. So, if you haven't yet experienced the power of the Spirit, all you have to do is ask. God is a Father who loves to give the Holy Spirit to those who ask him (Luke 11:11–13).

KEY 2: DEALING WITH REJECTION

Another key to enjoying the freedom of spiritual adoption concerns rejection. Rejection can be defined as a traumatic experience of abandonment resulting in the feeling of being unloved. Many people come into the kingdom of God carrying a baggage of rejection. Some were rejected before they were even born. Others experienced abandonment as babies or young children. Still more have experienced rejection later on in life—through separation, bereavement, hospitalization, abuse, shaming, humiliation, racism, disapproval, divorce, and so forth. Needless to say, such deep wounds cause people to surround their hearts with a hard, self-protective shell. In most cases, conversion results in the forgiveness of sins but not necessarily in the healing of every wound.

This is very much my own testimony. I was converted at the age of seventeen. The day I repented of my sins and confessed Jesus Christ as my Lord, I was justified by faith and born again by the Spirit of God. At that moment I received the loving Spirit of adoption. Tragically, I did not enter into the actual experience of being loved by Abba, Father until ten years later. For a long time I was saved but I was still sick.

I well remember the time when I began to get in touch with the buried trauma of rejection. I had been married to Alie for about three years when I began to suffer from the most vivid nightmares. These happened every night and in each case the scenario was the same—Alie rejecting me in favour of another man. These dreams were so real that it would take a lot of reassurance each morning before I would be ready to tackle the challenges of the day.

This awful situation continued unabated for about nine months. Eventually I went to visit my pastoral tutor at the theological college where I was training for the ordained ministry. I explained the difficulties I was experiencing and he arranged for me to see him for a number of counselling sessions. In each of these he didn't say much, but he allowed me to tell my story from the very beginning. As I spoke, the Holy Spirit gradually revealed the root cause of these dreams. I started to see that my problem was not some punishment for sins I had committed, but rather the long-term backlash of the trauma of being rejected by my natural parents and being placed in an orphanage. My tutor began to show me that there was a deep-seated separation anxiety in my life that needed to be confronted and removed. Only then would the nightmares stop and the fear of rejection go.

After the fourth session I felt ready to receive healing prayer with the laying on of hands. This was something totally new to me so I needed a considerable amount of reassurance. However, my tutor gently encouraged me and I subsequently began to prepare myself to receive ministry at the next healing service at the college chapel. I did this over a period of two or three weeks before the important day arrived. I still recall going for a long walk on the afternoon in question, and experiencing a tremendous wave of God's peace breaking upon me as I prayed my way down a country lane. I felt enfolded by God's love, comforted that I had nothing to fear from his touch, and reassured that all would be well.

That evening I went forward after receiving Communion and a number of friends gathered around me. As they welcomed the Holy Spirit and started praying for me, I had a vision of a place filled with pitch-black darkness. There I saw Jesus dying on the cross and shouting out to his Father, 'My God, my God, why have you abandoned me?' Instantly I understood that Jesus had entered into the very heart of what I was experiencing. I knew at once that he had taken upon himself my wounds as well as my sins. As that happened, I sensed a tremendous release.

Indeed, I would describe it as deliverance. From that moment on I have never had another nightmare about rejection. I have been freed from the tendency to manipulate people into proving that they love me and will not leave me. On top of that, I began to experience the true joy and intimacy of worshipping Abba, Father.

A key to experiencing the full release of the loving Spirit of adoption is to deal with any issues of rejection in our lives. The truth is that we cannot abandon ourselves into Abba's arms of love until we have had our past wounds healed. In other words, abandonment *to* God can only occur once we have been delivered from the trauma of our own abandonment *by* others. This necessarily involves remembering the hurtful episodes of our life-script. It may well involve narrating these painful events with a trusted, pastoral friend. It will certainly involve our asking the Holy Spirit to come into the locked places of our hearts in order to bring the light of God's revelation, the purity of his cleansing, and the fire of his love.

I would like to add that I regard it as immensely significant that my healing from rejection occurred during a Holy Communion service. The Lord's Supper was originally a Jewish Passover meal. The Passover *seder* to this day celebrates God's adoption of Israel as his chosen people and his rescue of them at the exodus. It is truly a liturgy of liberation commemorating the journey of Israel from slavery to sonship.

Jesus was a rabbi not a vicar. He was a Jew not a Gentile. He celebrated Passover not Easter. If we were to recover the Jewishness of the Lord's Supper, we would find that it is still a liturgy of liberation. We would discover that one of its primary themes is the new exodus of Jesus' death—an exodus that gave us our deliverance from slavery and our adoption into sonship. Focused as it is on the cross—the place where Jesus himself experienced a father's abandonment—we would find it to be a wonderful resource for the healing of our own experiences of rejection.

One vital key that unlocks the blessings of adoption is therefore the healing of rejection. When such healing comes, we begin to understand in our hearts the beauty and truth of Psalm 27:10: 'Though my father and mother reject me, the Lord will receive me.'

Key 3: Dealing with legalism

Another major key to unlocking the blessings of spiritual adoption is liberation from legalism (law-centred Christianity). Bob George has written that the contrast between grace and law is crucial not only to Paul's theology but also to our sense of God's acceptance. He writes:

There are only three possible answers [to the question, 'How can we be accepted by God'?]. Man is made (or tries to make himself) acceptable to God by law, by grace, or by a third, hybrid means called Galatianism.[59]

When Paul wrote his letter to the Galatians he was greatly disturbed by the way in which some of the Jewish believers were trying to impose a legalistic form of the faith on the church. They were attempting to persuade people that they needed to earn God's acceptance through the rigorous observance of Torah and other minute regulations. Paul was horrified by this. He knew full well that this kind of empty religiosity had been dealt a decisive blow by the Calvary love of God. He understood that a person only finds favour with God through believing in the finished work of the cross. When that happens, the love of law is replaced by the law of love. Instead of being driven by whips of legalism, a person is drawn into greater and greater obedience by the cords of God's gracious affection.

My own story may be helpful again at this point. After a short while as a new Christian, I came under the spell of a Christian man who infiltrated the school Christian Union. This person introduced a model of spiritual oversight known as 'heavy shepherding'. Using convincing arguments, he insisted that a number of us should make a pact in which we pledged total obedience and accountability to him. His demands were excessive in just about every respect. We were not allowed to watch a film without consulting him, and the slightest misdemeanours were met with discipline (based on Hebrews 12:4–11). Needless to say, this had a very damaging effect on me personally, and ultimately led to a number of new converts backsliding from the faith altogether.

Even in my relatively short time as a minister I have met many people who have had experiences like this. There is no one denomination or movement that is responsible for this pernicious aberration. It is a demonic deception that rears its ugly head in many contexts from time to time. In each situation the result is that believers start to see God as a punitive Judge who is all too ready to abuse them with the iron rod of discipline. They cannot see him as a Father whose adopting grace inspires holiness. In such contexts, the loving Spirit of adoption is seemingly absent and unwelcome. It is the letter of the law, not the life-giving Spirit, that matters most.

How, then, is this spell broken? In Galatians 3:10–14, Paul talks about the greatest deal in history. He speaks about the cross as the place where Jesus Christ receives our curses and where we receive God's blessing. In the first instance, Paul is thinking of one particular kind of curse being broken at Calvary—the curse of legalism. What particular blessing is Paul talking about? For him, it is the gift of the Spirit, which in turn brings us into the full realization of our adoption as sons and daughters. At the moment of believing in Jesus we experience an exodus in miniature. We are set free from all form of slavery (including hedonism and legalism) and we are led by one greater than Moses—the Lord Jesus—into the Promised Land of Abba's love. We then enter into the place of blessing promised to Abraham. For Paul, this blessing is charismatic; it is the promised gift of the Spirit. A few verses later, he will identify this as the Spirit who enables us to cry 'Abba, Father'.

When I came forward for ministry at that Communion Service at my theological college, I received a double blessing. Not only was my rejection healed through the power of the cross. The curse of legalism was broken as well. This paved the way for the release of the Spirit of adoption in my life, as it will for all of us. A vital key in our liberation into sonship is therefore deliverance from legalism. In the final analysis, the contrast between law and grace is the contrast between two antithetical means of experiencing God's acceptance, as Bob George has discovered. Law says, 'You have to earn it.' Grace says, 'You only need to believe in order to receive it.' If you have been exposed for any time to a legalistic distortion of the faith, then the effects of this will need to be broken through prayer. Then you will be free indeed to know God as a loving Father rather than a punishing slave-driver.

Having said that, we need to be realistic. Living by the Spirit will bring conflict as well as comfort. Stephen, the first Christian martyr, was a man 'full of God's grace and power' (Acts 6:8). In other words, he was a man who knew God accepted him on the basis of grace rather than law. Consequently he was filled with the dynamic power of the Holy Spirit. As he began to do great miracles in Jerusalem, his actions aroused opposition from 'members of the Synagogue of the Freedmen' (Acts 6:9)—in other words, from Jewish men who had been liberated from slavery. Do you see the irony here? Those who had been set free from physical slavery could not see their need to be freed from spiritual slavery. So they whipped Stephen with their verbal, demonic assault.

Redemption from the curse of legalism opens the door to the loving Spirit of adoption. It releases us from slavery into adopted sonship. That is the good news! The bad news is that becoming a Spirit-filled son or daughter is not a passport to a problem-free life. To those who are still in religious slavery, it will provoke jealousy, misunderstanding and opposition. When confronted by such people, the man or woman of the Spirit needs to exhibit the fruit of the Spirit. As an adopted son, he needs to behave like the Son by nature.

KEY 4: DEALING WITH FEAR

Another major key to experiencing the full joy of our adoption is deliverance from fear. In Romans 8:15, Paul says, 'You did not receive a spirit that makes you a slave again to fear, but you received the Spirit of adoption.' Paul is talking about two spirits here, an unholy spirit and the Holy Spirit. The unholy spirit afflicts the believer with doubt and uncertainty about his position before God. The Holy Spirit comforts the believer with the full assurance of sonship. The fruit of the unholy spirit is fear. The fruit of the Holy Spirit is love. The believer whose life is characterized by fear is described by Paul as a slave. The believer whose life is marked by love is called a son. The first sees God as a fearful Judge. The second sees him as a loving Father. The first is driven by the flesh to earn God's acceptance. The second is led by the Spirit into the knowledge of his acceptance. The first is constantly under condemnation and cries out in terror. The second basks in the Father's affection and cries out in praise, 'Abba, Father!' The first is bound. The second is truly free.

It is vital at this point to understand that demonic spirits are real. Paul is not referring to a psychological attitude when he speaks about 'the spirit that makes you a slave again to fear'. He is surely not speaking about God's Spirit either. No, Paul is talking about a demonic spirit that operates at the bidding of Satan, the accuser of the brethren. This spirit tries to seduce believers into a place of neurotic uncertainty about whether the Father loves them. It seeks to bewitch the children of God into striving to earn God's acceptance through legalism and ritualism. It besieges the believer's mind with lies that lead to a deep-seated insecurity in his relationship with God and with others. An unholy fear of God and of men begins to hold the believer captive. Until these chains of fear are broken through divine power, the believer will be under the 'stronghold' of unworthiness (2 Corinthians 10:4).

How do we get rid of this pernicious spirit of fear? The apostle John gives us the answer:

There is no fear in love. But perfect love drives out fear, because fear has to do with punishment. The one who fears is not made perfect in love.
1 JOHN 4:18

The Greek word *phobos*, translated 'fear' (and from which we get the word 'phobia'), is a servile fear that holds people captive to insecurity. It is a terror of divine punishment and rejection, particularly at the Last Judgment. The word 'love' refers primarily to God's love for us—a love which John calls 'perfect'. This adjective means 'complete in every way'. It means 'gracious, unmerited, all-consuming and faultless'.

John says that this perfect love 'drives out' fear. Exposure to the all-consuming passion of God causes the spirit of fear to be violently expelled from our hearts. The phrase 'drives out' is the same one that Jesus uses when he speaks about 'driving out' the prince of this world at Calvary (John 12:31). Clearly John is referring to an act of supernatural deliverance. As the believer is soaked in the fire of God's love, the spirit of fear is cast out. The result is that the believer no longer lives as a slave—a life marked by insecurity—but as a son. He no longer fears the presence of God. He relishes it!

A lot of the controversy surrounding the Toronto blessing centred on the issue of strong bodily reactions to the presence of the Holy Spirit. Some were critical of the leadership at the Toronto Airport Fellowship because they felt that the phenomena were caused by demons. John Arnott's response was this: 'It's possible. But the question is, are they coming or are they going?' From my own experience I have to say that some of the violent shaking experienced by people during this phase of renewal was certainly due to deliverance, and specifically to the driving out of the spirit of fear. When I visited the Toronto Airport Fellowship, I was exposed to a place where there was an extraordinary residential anointing. In other words, I came into a sacred space where God's empowering presence was manifestly at work. In that context, God poured out the fire of his perfect love in an extravagant and overwhelming manner. As a result, the spirit of fear was broken off many of us, and we came once again to a point where we were secure in our relationship with Abba, Father, and set free from the desperate desire to please others.

All those who want to enjoy the full liberty of adopted sonship will sooner or later need to face the issue of fear. God wants us to have a holy fear not an unholy fear. He also wants us to know his love and reciprocate with passionate love for him. Those who live daily in the experience of their spiritual adoption know that God is a Father who disciplines his children, so they work out their salvation in the kind of fear and trembling that leads to life. But above all they know that God is a glorious Father who accepts them on the basis of faith rather than works. As such, they rest secure in their position in Christ and resist the performance orientation with which the enemy has assaulted both the world and the church. Deliverance from the demonic spirit of fear is therefore a vital key. Once the chains of fear have been unlocked, we can start to build our self-worth on God's love for us, not on our ability to please others.

KEY 5: DEALING WITH UNFORGIVENESS

Another crucial key concerns unforgiveness. We may have been healed of the sense of rejection in our lives, but we need also to forgive those who rejected us. Until we have released others from our grief, anger and bitterness, then we will never experience the full liberty of sonship and daughterhood. Indeed, Paul makes it clear that such an unforgiving attitude grieves the Holy Spirit and gives the devil a foothold in our hearts (Ephesians 4:26–27, 30). Until this debilitating sin of unforgiveness is confessed and removed, there will always be a blockage in our hearts, preventing us from knowing the full measure of Abba's adopting grace. Dealing with unforgiveness is therefore critical.

In 1985 the Lord released me from the deep-seated separation anxiety that had been lurking in my life like a virus. As I received healing prayer, I was miraculously released from the nightmare of rejection. The pain of my abandonment as a baby left me at that moment. However, it wasn't until ten years later that I discovered that there was another vital key. At the 'Catch the Fire' Conference in 1995 I released my biological parents (particularly my father) from my anger at abandoning me. As that happened, I began to understand the power of forgiveness. Forgiveness was indeed the golden key that unlocked the chains that bound me. Interestingly, it set me free to love my own children with a demonstrative affection that I had not known before. It also released me as a church leader. I therefore received a fourfold liberation—in my relationship with my natural father, in my relationship as a father, in my relationship as a spiritual father (2 Corinthians 4:15) and in my relationship with my heavenly Father. No wonder John Arnott called the Toronto blessing 'the Father's blessing'!

It is said that God will not do a great work through us until he has done a great work *in* us. God wants us to move mountains through faith (Mark 11:23). That is the great work he wants to do *through* us. But the great work he wants to do *in* us has to do with the purification and healing of our hearts. That is why Jesus goes on to say, after his teaching on moving mountains, 'And when you stand praying, if you hold anything against anyone, forgive him, so that your Father in heaven may forgive you your sins' (Mark 11:25). If we want to be conduits of the life-changing love of God, then we must allow his Holy Spirit to cleanse us of the obstructions to the flow of his power.

Unforgiveness, as John Arnott teaches, is an energy-sapping force in our relationship with God and with others.[60] None of us will experience the glorious freedom of the adopted children of God until we have relinquished our anger with others and forgiven those who have rejected and abused us. No one is pretending that this is easy. For many it will involve a long process rather than a simple one-off event. Nevertheless, God is sovereign, and when we are ready and the time is right, he helps us to forgive and floods our hearts with the loving Spirit of adoption. As this occurs, the devil's foothold is displaced and we are equipped to fulfil our God-given destiny.

KEY 6: DEALING WITH SHAME

Many people have had terrible lies spoken over them. They have been told that they will never be any good, that they are worthless, and that they will never amount to anything. These pronouncements stick like labels. They humiliate people and cause them to believe that they are worthless.

This is what is meant by 'shame'. I once heard someone put it like this: 'The difference between guilt and shame is profound. Guilt says, "I've made a mistake." Shame says, "I am a mistake."' If a believer is to enter into the glorious freedom of adopted sonship, then all the issues of shame need to be confronted. The devil always brings condemnation. The Lord always brings conviction. Between condemnation and conviction there is a vast chasm. The first causes us to grovel in unworthiness. The second causes us to clean up our act so that the channel of love between God and us may be unpolluted.

One of the issues of shame in my own life had to do with illegitimacy. My biological parents were not married when Claire and I were born. Nor were they at any subsequent time. We therefore grew up with the stigma of illegitimacy. Not only did we carry the shame of being abandoned, we also carried the shame of being born out of wedlock. It also did not help that from time to time we were described to our faces as 'bastards' by people whom we loved and trusted. From these episodes I know the destructive power in words, particularly in the negative naming of others.

One of my favourite characters in the Gospels is Thomas. He missed out when the risen Jesus first appeared to the disciples in the upper room (John 20:19–23). He must have felt very excluded and rejected when he heard about this. Some of that pain comes out in his refusal to believe unless he himself sees and touches the risen Lord. This remark has led many preachers to name him as Doubting Thomas.

But what was it exactly that Thomas doubted? He surely did not doubt the fact that Jesus had risen from the dead! If we claim that, then we have to say that Thomas' view of the other disciples was very negative. It means that he was convinced they were indulging in a cruel hoax when they said that they had seen the risen Lord. An alternative solution must therefore be found. My conviction is that Thomas' problem was a crippling sense of personal unworthiness. This is visible in his dysfunctional behaviour in John 11:16, where he says, 'Let's go back to Judea and die with Jesus.' That sounds like the remark of a man who desperately wants to please others and earn their approval.

If Thomas suffered from self-doubt, then one of the reasons for this may have been that he was always named 'Didymus', the Twin, instead of Thomas. I have already referred to the power of naming. Claire and I were often described as 'the twins' when we were little. This was not helpful. It had the effect of obscuring our identities and undermining our God-given individuality. In Thomas' case, this nickname may have formed part of a root of shame in his life that led to self-doubt. If that is the case, then Thomas did not doubt the resurrection. Rather, he doubted that the risen Jesus would ever appear to him personally. In this respect he is the prototype of all those who doubt that the Holy Spirit would ever touch, heal and fill them personally. The underlying cause of this kind of scepticism is shame. It is the inner belief that one is not worthy to receive the honour of a personal visitation from God.

Jesus is very compassionate with Thomas. A week after his first appearance to the disciples, he makes a personal appearance to him. Thomas is invited to put his finger in the wounds of Jesus. He is being permitted a unique privilege here. At a figurative level, he is being allowed to enter into the suffering of the Saviour. These wounds included the labels and the harsh names that Jesus himself was given—such as Samaritan, demon-possessed, a mere man—and so on. As Thomas identifies at the closest level with the rejection experienced by Jesus, his own shame seems to dissipate like an early morning mist. He is set free to address Jesus as 'my Lord and my God'. The little pronoun 'my' reveals that Thomas is now secure in his relationship with the Lord. That relationship is personal, intimate and adoring.

The Bible says that it is 'by Christ's wounds that we have been healed' (1 Peter 2:24). As we receive a deeper revelation of the sufferings of Jesus, we find healing. In Thomas' case, healing came when he saw that Jesus had suffered the shame of humiliating labels. In my case, the healing of the effects of my illegitimacy came when I realized that Jesus himself was born out of wedlock. When this kind of shame is removed, space is made to receive the loving Spirit of adoption. Put another way, Jesus takes us into the dark room of our hearts and turns our negatives into positives. He transforms the lies of the enemy into the truths of God. We are given a proper sense of self-worth based on the word of God and the inner testimony of the Holy Spirit. This in turn sets us free to worship, as Thomas experienced.

KEY 7: DEALING WITH ADDICTION

In this therapy-oriented culture of ours, it is vital to remember that Jesus Christ died to save us from our sins, not just to heal us of our wounds. There is a major tendency in today's Western world to obscure the issue of sin by blaming our immoral behaviour on our past traumas. As Jay Adams beautifully puts it:

I went to my psychiatrist to be psychoanalysed
To find out why I killed the cat and blackened my husband's eyes.
He laid me down on a downy couch to see what he could find,
And here is what he dredged up from my subconscious mind:
When I was one, my mommie hid my dollie in a trunk,
And so it follows naturally that I am always drunk...

At three, I had the feeling of ambivalence toward my brothers,
And so it follows naturally I poison all my lovers.
But now I am happy; now I've learned the lesson
                                        this has taught;
That everything I do that's wrong is someone else's fault.[61]

However destructive our past history has been, we cannot completely relinquish our individual responsibility. We cannot wholly blame our sinful words and actions on those who have hurt us, nor on the devil who tempts us. We have been given the precious gift of free will. We therefore choose whether or not to commit a sin. We decide whether or not to follow a path that pleases self or pleases God.

One of the major obstacles to receiving the loving Spirit of adoption is the presence of sin—particularly habitual sin—in our lives. A better term for habitual sin is 'addiction'. Now I have written extensively on this subject elsewhere,[62] so at this point a brief definition will have to do. Addiction is essentially a process whereby my life becomes more and more controlled by a habit that enhances my moods and on which I become destructively and excessively dependent. Some addictions are simply symptoms of greed. In other words, they are purely the result of a self-indulgent streak in our fallen humanity. However, most addictions are symptoms of a deep, inner pain. In other words, they develop because of a fundamental love-hunger which we try to fill using food, cigarettes, sex, relationships, coffee, work, success, whatever. In neither case can a person blame their addiction on a force outside themselves. The person who becomes an addict because of greed cannot blame the devil. A person who becomes an addict because of pain cannot blame their parents. The decision to find help from a mood-altering habit rather than the Living God is our choice and ours alone. In the final analysis, this is a decision about what to worship. The addict chooses to worship something or someone other than God. That is idolatry.

The woman of Samaria was an addict (John 4:4–42). She had been married to five men and was living now with a sixth. Today we would call her a 'relationship addict'. In other words, she was seeking to satisfy the hole in her soul through dependent relationships with men. When she met Jesus, she met her Saviour. He introduced her to the glorious Father and encouraged her to worship him in spirit and in truth. The word used for 'worship' here is the Greek verb *proskuneo*, and this literally means 'to approach someone in order to kiss'. This is deeply significant. It means that Jesus addresses the core of the woman's addiction head on. He recognizes that her addiction to relationships (and probably also to sex) is a symptom of love-hunger. He also knows that an addiction is a misuse of the God-given desire to worship. It involves worshipping something created rather than the Creator. So he redirects her attention to the perfect Abba who will never leave nor forsake her, and he intro-duces her to a *proskuneo*-centred relationship with him. In the process, the way is open for her to confess her sin, receive healing for her addiction, and to become an adopted daughter of the Living God. Put another way, the hand of divine love reaches down to her at her level, thereby giving her the opportunity to turn from a prostitute into a princess.

If we are to enjoy the glorious freedom of the adopted children of God, then the blockages need to be removed from our lives. The obstructions of deception, rejection, legalism, fear, unforgiveness and shame need to go. So does the problem of habitual sin, or addiction. Abba, Father is looking for pure, undivided, worshipful hearts.

We therefore can't have joyful intimacy without rigorous purity. In 2 Timothy 2:19, Paul describes the foundation of the church. On the foundation stones there are two inscriptions. The first has to do with intimacy: 'The Lord knows those who are his.' As always, the verb 'know' denotes personal heart-knowledge, not merely intellectual, propositional understanding. The second has to do with purity: 'Every-one who confesses the name of the Lord must turn away from wickedness'. Here God calls us to a radical, daily repentance or turning from sin. The two things that Jesus Christ—the true foundation of the church—has given are intimacy with God and purity through repentance. Both are important. If we only stress intimacy with God, then the danger is that we will end up with an overly emotional Christianity where there is plenty of room for the Spirit but not enough room for the cross. If we only stress purity with God, then the danger is that we will end up with an overly cerebral, cold and cheerless

Christianity where there is plenty of room for the cross but not enough room for the Spirit.[63]

Tom Smail has written a seminal book entitled *The Forgotten Father*. In it he wrote briefly about the doctrine of adoption and pointed to the significance of Romans 8:17, where Paul exhorts the adopted children of God to share in the sufferings of the Son of God. Smail warned those in the charismatic renewal of the dangers of neglecting the call to obedience and purity. He said:

It will relapse into sentimentality and chumminess with a heavenly Daddy who is seen as the distributor of goodies, unless it is constantly disciplined by the fear of the Lord that was at the heart of Jesus' practice of his own Sonship.[64]

Purity and intimacy therefore go together. Those who are the children of God share in the Son's sufferings by cultivating a life of obedience. But they also share in the Son's glory, the glory of knowing God as 'Abba, Father', not just now, but—after the General Resurrection—for eternity.

THE GLORIOUS FREEDOM OF THE CHILDREN OF GOD

Paul writes that one day the whole cosmos is going to be set free from its bondage to decay and brought into that glorious freedom enjoyed by the adopted children of God. He also writes that the creation waits in eager expectation for the adopted sons of God to be revealed. There is therefore a huge call upon our lives as believers. The polluted planet, the war-torn nations, the dispossessed refugees, the materially destitute, the fatherless children and the racially oppressed are all waiting with keen anticipation for God's adopted children to be fully made manifest. Spiritual adoption is therefore a blessing for the individual believer, yes, but it is also far, far more than that. Through believers like you and me, the whole earth is going to be blessed. As God's adopting grace becomes more and more visible in more and more of us, so every part of God's creation will say, 'We want to come into the orbit of that kind of love! Show us the way.' As we become more and more filled with the life of the Spirit, so a dying world will say, 'Help us to live.' As we become increasingly released from slavery and at the same time liberated into sonship, so the whole earth will cry, 'Show us how to unlock these oppressive chains.' Never forget: the blessings of adoption are initially individual but ultimately cosmic.

As we wait eagerly for the climax of our adoption—the redemption of our bodies on the Last Day—God calls us to pray. He wants the Holy Spirit to gather us up into the intercession of the Son of God, who is right now interceding at the right hand of Abba, Father in heaven. He wants his Spirit to pray through his adopted sons and daughters with the compassionate, heartfelt groans of heaven. Abba, Father wants his sons and daughters to nurture a life of travailing prayer. Those whom he has chosen and adopted are to pray that the whole world will accept the invitation into God's covenant of love. The doors of the Father's house are opened wide. The world is saying, 'Show us the way to go home.' Who will answer the question? The adopted sons and daughters of the Living God. We are the hope of the world.

CONCLUSION

From Orphans to Heirs

There is a passage of scripture that's read out at just about every funeral service. It is John 14:1–6, in which Jesus promises his disciples that he is going ahead to prepare a place for them in the Father's house. I often wonder, as I'm reading these words, how much assurance of this truth my listeners really have. Sometimes I wonder how sure I am that I'm going to spend eternity in Abba's house. Someone once asked the following: 'Are you afraid of dying? Or are you homesick for the Father's house in heaven?' That is a sobering question, and one that tests the level of our assurance of salvation.

This book has been a celebration of the great but neglected truth of our spiritual adoption. The Bible teaches that those who believe in Jesus Christ receive the loving Spirit of adoption and become the sons and daughters of the Living God. Adoption is therefore intimately connected with assurance. Those who live as sons will be sure of their heavenly home, while those who live as slaves can never really be certain. As Jesus put it in John 8:34–35:

I tell you the truth, everyone who sins is a slave to sin. Now a slave has no permanent place in the family, but a son belongs to it for ever.

OUR FUTURE INHERITANCE

Paul teaches us that our spiritual adoption not only makes us sons, but it also makes us heirs—co-heirs indeed with Jesus Christ (the Son by nature). This means that there is a future dimension to our adoption. It shows that our adoption as sons and daughters will be fully realized on the Last Day when the Son returns on the clouds and raises us to life at the General Resurrection.

Paul underlines this truth in Romans 8:23, a passage in which he explores life between the first and the second comings of Christ. He writes, 'We ourselves, who have the firstfruits of the Spirit, groan inwardly as we wait eagerly for our adoption as sons, the redemption of our bodies.'

At first sight this looks confusing. Has Paul not said that we are already adopted through the work of the Spirit in our hearts (Romans 8:15)? Yes he has, but adoption is a three-dimensional truth. Adoption first of all brings freedom from slavery (the past). It secondly provides us with a new status as sons and daughters of the Living God (the present). It thirdly gives us the great hope of eternal life with the Father in heaven (the future).

When Paul speaks of the future dimension of adoption he is referring to what he calls 'the redemption of our bodies' (Romans 8:23). In other words, when we are eventually raised from death at the Second Coming of Jesus, we will receive new resurrection bodies. Our old bodies will be redeemed. Only then will we fully enter into our adoption as sons and daughters. Only then will we be granted total liberty from creation's bondage to decay and brought into the glorious freedom of the children of God (Romans 8:21). Only then will the sons and daughters of God be revealed (Romans 8:19). As Packer has put it:

This, the blessing of resurrection day, will make actual what was implicit in the relationship of adoption, for it will introduce us into the full experience of the heavenly life now enjoyed by our elder brother.[65]

THE CROWN OF EVERLASTING LIFE

During the course of this book I have made reference to my adoptive father's death. He died on 17 January 1997 after a long struggle with Parkinson's disease. During those years, he had become a shadow of his former self. He had become gaunt, forgetful, incontinent and often incoherent. It was desperately sad to see his body deteriorating before our very eyes.

In the last year of his life, the family made the difficult decision to stop nursing Dad at home and have him placed in residential care. My mother Joy had borne the brunt of the home-care and was absolutely exhausted.

When the sad day came, we left Dad in a lovely nursing home run by a religious order just outside Norwich.

During the following months, my mother faithfully visited Dad every day. She would drive over, stay for four or five hours, and then say farewell. The goodbyes were the hardest. Sometimes Dad would grasp hold of Mum's wedding ring and beg her not to leave. She would eventually go, but would spend the journey home weeping.

In January 1997, Dad developed severe complications and was transferred to the Norfolk and Norwich hospital. Overnight he became worse, and we were told that he would not live for more than twenty-four hours. The following day, a Friday, he died in my brother's arms at 3.00pm. I had prayed for him at his bedside and read from the Scriptures (Psalm 23). When I had said 'goodbye', my brother Giles insisted that I said, 'Au revoir—until we see each other again.'

A week later we gathered in a crematorium just outside Norwich for Dad's funeral. It was a dull, overcast and drizzly day. There were only seven of us there because we wanted it to be a private occasion. My mum sat on the front row of the chapel, with Giles and me on either side of her. She looked desperately unhappy. For a whole year she had looked so sad and lonely. Her furrowed brow and wounded eyes were distressing to look at.

But in the middle of the vicar's address, something happened. Her facial expression totally changed from one of mourning to one of serene calm and even happiness. At the time I remember thinking how strange that was. Though it had been excellent, I couldn't personally see anything in the service that might have produced such a profound transformation.

Later we gathered for a cup of tea at home. During a lull in the conversation, my mum suddenly asked, 'Did you see it?'

'Did we see "what"?' we replied.

'During the vicar's sermon, a shaft of light came from behind me and illuminated the part of the coffin where Dad's head was. As that happened, I saw a crown descending towards that point. I remembered the words at my confirmation as a child, "Be thou faithful unto death and I will give thee the crown of everlasting life." As I recalled that verse, I heard a little voice saying, "Dad has won his crown."'

FROM ORPHANS TO HEIRS

That story is remarkable as well as encouraging because my mother would say that she is neither evangelical nor charismatic. Yet at a critical moment in her bereavement, the Holy Spirit gave her a vision and spoke a word of resurrection hope into her heart, 'Dad has won his crown.' Consequently, we all felt that for Dad, the best is yet to be.

Paul talks about adoption in the future as well as the past and present tenses. The future tense of adoption has to do with 'the redemption of our bodies' at the General Resurrection. When that great day comes, those who have become the children of God will receive new bodies which will never decay. Like Jesus—the firstborn from among the dead—we will be raised immortal, and the whole of creation will see that we are indeed sons and daughters of the Living God. In short, as co-heirs with Christ, we will inherit what Jesus inherited—resurrection bodies!

Here again we see something of the amazing grace of God. In my own family, I have always been struck by my parents' generosity towards Claire and me. They have consistently stressed that they look upon us with the same degree of devotion as Giles and that they do not distinguish between their natural son and their adopted children. In relation to our inheritance, they have made this particularly clear by emphasizing that Claire and I will be equal co-heirs with Giles. While in material terms this does not amount to very much, in emotional terms it amounts to a lot. I have always been deeply moved by the thought that I, as an adopted son, stand to inherit exactly the same as Giles, the son by nature.

So it is with our heavenly Father. Once we are adopted into God's family, we become sons and daughters of God. God's word stresses that we are no longer slaves but sons, no longer orphans but co-heirs with our older Brother, Jesus. Just as he inherited a crown of everlasting life, so will we. The 'crown' of Revelation 2:10 is the victor's laurel crown given to the winning athlete in the ancient games. If we keep running the race of faith until the end of our lives, looking to Jesus who has already finished, then we will inherit an everlasting crown and we will receive redeemed, resurrected bodies. In other words, we will inherit what Jesus inherited.

The key, then, is to remain focused on Jesus, the Son by nature, and to be conformed to his likeness. Through the power of the Spirit we need to become more and more like Jesus, developing the family likeness. Only those who have the Son in their lives stand to inherit resurrection bodies. Perhaps, in conclusion, a story says it best:

Years ago there was a wealthy man, a widower who, together with his only son, shared a passion for art. Together they travelled the world adding only the finest treasures to their collection.

One autumn, war engulfed the nation and the young man left to serve his country. After only a few short weeks his father received a telegram. His beloved son was missing in action.

He anxiously awaited more news and, within days, his fears were confirmed. The young man had died while helping a wounded man. Distraught and lonely, the old man faced the coming Christmas period with sadness.

On Christmas morning, a knock at the door awakened the old man from his depression. At the door stood a soldier with a large package in his hand who introduced himself—'I was a friend of your son—the one he was rescuing when he died. May I come in for a few moments? I have something for you.'

As they began to talk, the soldier told how the man's son had spoken about their love of fine art. 'I'm an artist,' said the soldier, 'and I want to give you this.' As the old man unwrapped the package, the paper gave way to reveal a portrait of his son. Though the world would never consider it the work of a genius, the painting featured the young man's face in striking detail.

Overcome with emotion, the old man thanked the soldier, promising to hang the picture above the fireplace. Then he sat in his chair and spent Christmas gazing at the gift he had been given, which soon became his most prized possession. The following Spring, the old man became ill and passed away. The art world was in anticipation. According to his will, all the old man's works of art were to be auctioned on Christmas Day, the day he had received his greatest gift. Collectors from around the world gathered to bid on some of the world's most spectacular paintings.

But the auction began with a painting that was not on any museum's list. It was the painting of the old man's son. The auctioneer asked for an opening bid. The room was silent. 'Who will open the bidding with £100?' the auctioneer asked. Minutes passed. No one spoke.

From the back of the room someone voiced what many were thinking, 'Who cares about that painting? It's just a picture of his son. Let's forget it and go on to the good stuff.' More voices echoed in agreement. 'No, we have to sell this one first,' replied the auctioneer. 'Now, who will take the son?'

Finally, a friend of the old man spoke. 'Will you take fifty pounds for the painting? That's all I have. I knew the boy, so I'd like to have it.'

'I have fifty pounds. Will anyone go higher?' called the auctioneer. More silence. 'Going once, going twice, gone!' The gavel fell. Cheers filled the room and someone exclaimed: 'Now we can get on with it and bid on these treasures!' But the auctioneer announced that the auction was over.

Disbelief stunned the room. 'What do you mean, it's over? We didn't come here for a picture of some old guy's son. What about all of these paintings? There are millions of pounds worth of art here!'

'It's very simple,' the auctioneer replied. 'According to the will of the father, whoever takes the son gets it all!'[66]

NOTES

1   J. Packer, *Knowing God* (Hodder & Stoughton, 1993 edition), p.232.

2   Packer, *Knowing God*, p.232.

3   D. Theron, '"Adoption" in the Pauline Corpus', *Evangelical Quarterly* 28, p.8.

4   I was given this marvellous quotation by my friend Marc Dupont, who had sadly lost the exact source in Tozer's writings.

5   A. Outler and R. Heitzenrater (eds), *John Wesley's Sermons* (Abingdon Press, 1991 edition), p.134. The sermon quoted (and which will be frequently referred to during the course of this book) is 'The Spirit of Bondage and of Adoption' (Sermon 9, 1746).

6   J.M. Scott, *Adoption as Sons of God* (Tübingen, Mohr, 1992). Scott's book is the most thorough academic study of Paul's concept of adoption to date. While differing on matters of detail from Scott, I want to express my indebtedness to him here.

7   M. Stibbe, *Thinking Clearly About Revival* (Monarch, 1998), pp. 4–26.

8   I haven't said much about the gift of tongues in this book because I have written about the relationship between tongues and the Spirit of adoption in *Explaining Baptism in the Holy Spirit* (Sovereign World Ltd, 1995), p.46. The gift of tongues is essentially an adorational gift. Through it we are set free to adore Abba, Father with words given by the Spirit. As I have written in *Know Your Spiritual Gifts*, tongues-speech is 'the jubilate of an enraptured soul'.

9   J. Dunn, *The Theology of Paul the Apostle* (T&T Clark, 1998), p.437.

10   Packer, *Knowing God*, p.233.

11   C. Pinnock, *The Flame of Love: A Theology of the Holy Spirit* (IVP, 1996), p.149.

12   Packer, *Knowing God*, p.258.

13   See Scott's *Adoption as Sons of God*, Chapter 1.

14   I need to stress that the adoption of a slave within one's own household was only one possible adoption scenario among a number in the Graeco-Roman world of the first century. However, the adoption of slaves was not uncommon. As I.A.H. Combes puts it, 'The slave of the ancient world might, and many did, obtain freedom from (and even adoption by) their masters'. *The Metaphor of Slavery in the Writings of the Ancient Church*, (Sheffield Academic Press, 1998), p.69.

15   R. Hammerton-Kelly, *God the Father: Theology and Patriarchy in the Teaching of Jesus* (Fortress Press, 1979). Hammerton-Kelly writes, 'In order to express this new and characteristically Mosaic theology, the Yahwists chose the image of adoption. The relationship between God and his people is that of father and adopted son' (p.31). For the idea that the exodus marks the moment of Israel's election and adoption, see pp.35 and 50.

16   Joseph, Jacob's son, was sold into slavery by his wicked brothers. In Egypt he was raised by the Pharaoh to a place of great honour. His father and his brothers subsequently came to Egypt to beg for help during a time of great famine. Joseph eventually revealed himself to them as Jacob's son and their long-lost brother. This could be seen as a type of the journey from slavery to sonship.

17   S. Storms, *God's Passion for You* (Kingsway, 1998), p.44. Sam has been greatly influenced by John Piper's writings, particularly by Piper's emphasis on enjoying God for who he is.

18   H. Hanegraaff, *Christianity in Crisis* (Nelson Word Ltd, 1993), pp. 147–51.

19   In classical theology, the idea that God suffers has been a no-go area. Heavily influenced as it was by Greek philosophy, Christian theology spoke of the 'impassibility' of God and accused people of

'patri-passianism' if they spoke of the Father's pain. Happily, the work of theologians such as Jürgen Moltmann (amongst many other post-Auschwitz writers) has put paid to this.

20 S. Townend, 1995, Kingsway's Thankyou Music/MCPS.

21 B. Manning, *Abba's Child: The Cry of the Heart for Intimate Belonging* (NavPress, 1994), pp.86–9.

22 P. Yancey, *What's So Amazing About Grace?* (Zondervan, 1997) p.70.

23 Adoptionism (sometimes also known as 'dynamic Monarchianism') taught that Jesus Christ was a mere man upon whom God's Spirit descended at his baptism. The first person to propose this view was a Byzantine leather-merchant known as Theodotus, and he is said to have preached it in Rome in AD190. His views were later taken up by another Theodotus (this time a banker) in the third century, also in Rome. The most famous proponent of the Adoptionist position was Paul of Samosata, and his views were outlawed at the Synod of Antioch in AD268. The early church rightly condemned Adoptionism (which was only ever a fringe movement in Christianity) for undermining the doctrine of the Trinity, for if Jesus was only Son of God by adoption (i.e. for three years), then he could not be regarded as the Second Person of the eternal Godhead.

24 J. Jeremias, *The Prayers of Jesus* (SCM Press Ltd, 1967), Chapter 1 (pp.11–65).

25 J. Barr, '"Abba" isn't "Daddy"', *Journal of Theological Studies* 39, 1988, pp.28–47.

26 G. Fee, *God's Empowering Presence: The Holy Spirit in the Letters of Paul*, Hendrickson: Peabody, MS: 1994, p.411.

27 See Hammerton-Kelly, *God the Father*, p.72: 'The astonishing fact that in all five layers of the gospel tradition (Mark, Q, Matthew, Luke, and John) Jesus, with one exception [the cry from the cross in Mark 15:34], always invokes God as "Father" in his recorded prayers, directs our attention to the prayers... The term Jesus used

is the Aramaic "Abba" (stress on the second syllable) as its quotation in Mark 14:36 (the Gethsemane prayer) and its use by Paul (Romans 8:15; Galatians 4:6) show. The only reason why Mark and Paul, who were writing for Gentiles who knew no Aramaic, would quote this unintelligible word, is the undeniable tradition that it was indeed Jesus' special name for God.'

28 Some would prefer me to say that the Son became 'like' a slave. However, Paul says in Philippians 2:7 that Jesus 'took the very nature (*morphe*) of a slave'. The same expression is used in verse 6, where Jesus is described as being 'in very nature' (*morphe*) God'. If I am asked to translate the expression, 'Jesus became *like* a slave', then I have to translate the other expression, 'Jesus was *like* God'. No one would want me to do that! A second criticism that is sometimes made is this: Isn't the NIV correct to say that the Son became a 'servant' rather than a 'slave'? While *doulos* can be translated 'servant', its alternative translation ('slave') is surely correct in the context of a letter to a Roman congregation. The full force of the word *doulos* shouldn't be watered down. Paul is saying that Jesus Christ, the eternal Son of God, became a slave—the lowest form of life in the Roman Empire. My translation does this shocking thought more justice.

29 Packer, *Knowing God*, p.244.

30 See the unsurpassed discussion of this in Martin Hengel's classic work, *Crucifixion* (translated from the German by John Bowden, SCM Press Ltd, 1977 version). Chapter 8 is entitled 'The Slave's Punishment' (pp.51–56).

31 Taken from the *Anglican Hymn Book* (Church Book Room Press Ltd, 1966 edition), Hymn 383.

32 Quoted in Manning, *Abba's Child*, p.56.

33 E. Nesbitt, *The Railway Children* (Parragon Books, 1993 edition (first published in 1906)), pp.179–80.

34 Ishmael, Kingsway's Thankyou Music, 1984.

35 Quoted in J. Armstrong, *Five Great Evangelists* (Christian Focus Publications, 1997), pp.132–33.

36 P. Widdicombe, *The Fatherhood of God from Origen to Athanasius* (Clarendon Press, 1994), p.99.

37 Widdicombe, *The Fatherhood of God*, p.88.

38 R. Lovelace, *Dynamics of Spiritual Life: An Evangelical Theology of Renewal* (Paternoster Press, 1979), p.19.

39 Packer, *Knowing God*, p.226.

40 J. Arnott, *Keep the Fire* (Marshall Pickering, 1997), p.14.

41 Arnott, *Keep the Fire*, p.29.

42 Outler and Heitzenrater, *John Wesley's Sermons*, p.133, trace this typology of the human condition back to Augustine. Gregory Nazianzus also used it. He wrote, 'There are three classes among the saved: the slaves, the hired servants, the sons. If you are a slave, fear the whip; if you are a hired servant, expect only your wages; if you are more than this, a son, honour him as a father, and do that which is good, because it is good to obey a father; and even though no reward might come of it, it is a reward in itself, that you should please your father' (*Oration* 40.8).

43 Outler & Heitzenrater, *John Wesley's Sermons*, p.135.

44 Outler & Heitzenrater, *John Wesley's Sermons*, p.137.

45 Outler & Heitzenrater, *John Wesley's Sermons*, p.141.

46 Outler & Heitzenrater, *John Wesley's Sermons*, p.134.

47 Outler & Heitzenrater, *John Wesley's Sermons*, p.397. From Wesley's second sermon on 'The Witness of the Spirit' (Sermon 11, 1767). The first sermon had been published in 1746.

48 Outler & Heitzenrater, *John Wesley's Sermons*, p.138.

49   Quoted in the anthology *Fathers*, edited by Robert Backhouse (Kingsway, 1996).

50   C. Spurgeon, *On Revival*, p.26.

51   This prophetic word is attributed to Paul Cain.

52   C. Spurgeon, *On Revival*, p.27.

53   C. Spurgeon, *On Revival*, p.27.

54   F. Lake, *Clinical Theology: A Theological and Psychiatric Basis to Clinical Pastoral Care* (Darton, Longman & Todd, 1966), pp.204–207. I am indebted to Canon Robert Warren for first introducing me to Lake's Cycle of Well-Being.

55   The idea of the Christian as a 'noble slave' emerges in the writings of the church Fathers. The reason for this is that Paul occasionally speaks of the Christian life as a form of slavery (Romans 14:18). The apostles referred to themselves as God's slaves (Acts 4:29). Some of the Fathers found this strange, especially in the light of Paul's teaching that we have been rescued from slavery and been given the status of adopted sonship (see Origen's *Commentary on Paul's Epistle to the Romans* 1.1). Two solutions were given to this problem of apparent inconsistency in Paul's writings. Gregory of Nyssa teaches that God doesn't want any Christian to be a slave (*Against Eunomius* 10.4), and that the metaphor of slavery is now irrelevant. Others taught that Paul spoke of two forms of spiritual slavery, one negative (the slave to sin, or the slave to law), the other positive (the noble slave of Christ). Jerome spoke of the noble slavery that leads to love, as opposed to the ignoble slavery that leads to fear (see *Homily on Titus* PL 26.555C–556A).

56   J. Edwards, *Religious Affections* (The Banner of Truth Trust, 1994 edition), p.164.

57   Philip Stibbe, *Return Via Rangoon* (Leo Cooper, 1994 edition), pp. 215–16.

58   For more on this, see Widdicombe, *The Fatherhood of God*.

59   Bob George, *Classic Christianity* (Harvest House Publishers, Inc. 1989), p.123.

60   J. Arnott, *Explaining Forgiveness* (Sovereign World, 1998).

61   Jay Adams, *Competent to Counsel* (Baker Book House, 1970), p.8.

62   See my book, *O Brave New Church: Rescuing the Addictive Culture* (Darton, Longman & Todd, 1995).

63   It is so interesting to my mind that there are two major places of pilgrimage in the charismatic and pentecostal constituency today. One is Toronto and the other is Pensacola. Toronto is a place where intimacy with God is the main emphasis. Here the Lord has poured out the loving Spirit of adoption, refreshing believers, and enabling them to walk in God's love and give it away. Pensacola, on the other hand, is very different. Here purity with God is the main emphasis. Here the Lord has poured out the Spirit who convicts the world of its guilt in relation to sin, righteousness and judgment. Thousands have repented and got right with God at the altars of that church. In Toronto, the love of God governs the spiritual atmosphere. In Pensacola, it is the fear of the Lord.

It is the same Holy Spirit in both places. In Pensacola, the Holy Spirit is working powerfully for the justification of sinners. Here God is taking people back to the basic truth that 'everyone who confesses the name of the Lord must turn away from wickedness.' In Toronto, the Holy Spirit is working powerfully for the spiritual adoption of believers. Here God is taking people back to the basic truth that 'he knows those who are his', and he knows them intimately. Imagine a church where both of these emphases are joined together in a holy equilibrium! Imagine a church where there is both holy fear *and* passionate love. Imagine a church where there is equal emphasis on justification and adoption—where believers know both the foundational and the highest blessings of the gospel! Maybe this is the kind of church Luke is describing in Acts 9:31, when he says, 'Encouraged by the Holy Spirit, it grew in numbers, living in the fear of the Lord.'

64 T. Smail, *The Forgotten Father* (Hodder & Stoughton, 1980), p.147.

65 Packer, *Knowing God,* p.245.

66 Quoted in *Joy* Magazine, Assemblies of God in Great Britain and Ireland Inc., Issue no. 51, December 1998, p.12.

Appendix 1: Adoption and Redemption

Redemption literally means 'to buy something back'. In the context of the Roman slave trade in the ancient world, it meant 'to purchase someone out of slavery'. Thomas Wiedemann's classic study, *Greek and Roman Slavery* (Routledge, 1981), shows the many and varied ways in which such 'redemption' or 'manumission' took place. In the world of the New Testament, buying people out of slavery was a common practice and was regarded as an act of mercy. 'Redemption' therefore came readily to Paul's mind as he considered the mystery of the cross. In the same passage that he mentions the Father predestining us for adoption, Paul speaks about Jesus Christ as the one 'in whom we have redemption (*apolutrosis*) through his blood, the forgiveness of sins' (Ephesians 1:7). Clearly adoption and redemption are related concepts in Paul's mind. What then is the relationship between them?

In this book I am proposing that Paul thought of Christ's saving work as an event in which we are delivered from slavery and adopted into sonship. The concept of redemption fits nicely into that overall framework. When he uses the idea of redemption, Paul focuses on our deliverance from slavery and the means by which we are liberated. Thus, for Paul, Jesus Christ is the one who pays the redemption money, not with gold or silver but with his blood. He stresses in Ephesians 1:7 that our redemption is 'through Christ's blood'. The purpose of this redemption is described in Ephesians 1:7 as 'the forgiveness of sins'. Through Christ's substitutionary sacrifice, the debt of sin has been cancelled once and for all!

Redemption is therefore one aspect of our spiritual adoption. Adoption is an image which describes the whole story of our journey from slavery to sonship. This journey can be undertaken because of the work of the Father (who predestined us in love for adoption), the work of the Son (who died that the adoption price might be paid) and the work of the Spirit (who makes real in our subjective experience what has been achieved at Calvary).

While adoption focuses on the whole of the Trinity, redemption focuses on the work of the Son. In other words, it is Jesus who takes centre-stage in the image of redemption. The image of redemption throws the emphasis on the person of the Son, who paid the price that we might be bought out of slavery and given the awesome privilege of adopted sonship.

Also, while adoption focuses on a continuing relationship with Abba (embracing the past, the present and the future), redemption focuses on the unique act that has made this relationship possible in the first place. In other words, redemption highlights the shedding of Jesus' blood at Calvary. Redemption is therefore the means by which we can enter into adopted sonship. As Paul put it:

But when the time had fully come, God sent his Son, born of a woman, born under law, to redeem *those under law, that we might receive adoption.*
GALATIANS 4:4–5 (MY EMPHASIS)

Notice the important word 'that'. Jesus Christ redeemed us 'in order that' we might receive our adoption as daughters and sons. Christ's redeeming sacrifice is the one-off act that brings us into intimate relationship with Abba. There are therefore some similarities between adoption and redemption.

But the major differences are these: adoption is the whole story, redemption is part of the story. Adoption focuses on the role of the Father, the Son and the Spirit, while redemption focuses on the role of the Son. Adoption describes our ongoing relationship with the Father, while redemption describes the means by which this relationship of intimacy came into being.

One final point of contrast needs to be made. While adoption throws the spotlight on what we are saved *to* (our new relationship with Abba), redemption sheds light on what we are saved *from* (oppression by Satan). This becomes clear when we consider the difficult question, to whom is the redemption money paid? If redemption is understood as an aspect of adoption, then the answer is clear. The payment is made to Satan, the one who formerly held us under his *patria potestas*. The images of adoption and redemption imply a payment, and this was made to the one who formerly held us captive.

This means that the church Fathers who viewed Christ's death as a ransom to Satan—and their names include heavyweights like Origen, Gregory of Nyssa, Augustine, and Gregory the Great—may not have been as off the mark as subsequent theologians like to suggest. Of course, ridiculous aberrations are clearly visible in 'ransom' theology and these have been rightly exposed. Yet no one can deny that Jesus' death on the cross is a victorious act of deliverance in which we are redeemed from slavery and adopted into sonship. The ransom theory may have been crude, but there is a truth there that needs reclaiming, and this book on spiritual adoption may have gone some way towards doing that by showing that we have been delivered from the *patria potestas* of Satan.

APPENDIX 2: ADOPTION AND REGENERATION

Another question I am often asked is this, 'How does the concept of adoption relate to the idea of regeneration (being "born again" or "born from above")?' Here again we must define our terms carefully. Adoption, as we have seen, describes the bestowal of a gift of intimate relationship with the Living God. Regeneration, on the other hand, is that work of grace in our hearts that enables us to repent of our sins, confess Jesus as Lord, and pass from spiritual death to life. While adoption describes the gift of a continuing relationship of intimacy with Abba, Father (a relationship that is to last for eternity), regeneration describes the first stages at which we enter into this wonderful relationship.

Regeneration or rebirth occurs whenever an unbeliever is so impacted by the Spirit of God that she confesses her rebellion against God, receives forgiveness of sins, and enters the kingdom of God. At that moment, new life—life in all its fullness—is truly begun. At that moment, a person passes from spiritual death and is quickened by the Holy Spirit to enjoy the life of the Age to Come. Regeneration is therefore an event that enables us to become the children of God. It involves baptism in water but cannot be said to be the same as water baptism (a mistake made by many of the Fathers). It is related to our justification by faith—the means by which we are made righteous before God—but cannot be said to be the same as justification (a mistake made by some medieval theologians). Regeneration is like natural birth. It happens once and it results in the beginning of new life—the superabundant life that Jesus came to bring us (John 10:10). It is a work of divine grace not an act of human endeavour.

What then is the exact relationship between adoption (*huiothesia*) and regeneration (*palingenesia*)? In Titus 3:4–6, Paul writes the following:

But when the kindness and love of God our Saviour appeared, he saved us, not because of righteous things we had done, but because of his mercy. He saved us through the washing of rebirth and renewal by the Holy Spirit, whom he poured out on us generously through Jesus Christ our Saviour, so that, having been justified by his grace, we might become heirs having the hope of eternal life.

Here we see Paul speaking of what J.B. Phillips calls 'the cleansing power of the new birth'. The word 'washing' links rebirth with baptism in water, though water baptism should be understood here as an outward sign of an inner quickening caused by God's grace. The words 'renewal by the Holy Spirit' point to a vital dimension of regeneration, namely the fulfillment of God's promise to give his people a new heart and a new spirit (Ezekiel 36:26). The emphasis on a *new* heart and a *new* spirit reminds us that regeneration is the impartation of *new* life to those who are spiritually dead in their trespasses.

Here we see the difference between regeneration and adoption. Regeneration is linked with our initiation into the kingdom of God. Jesus said to Nicodemus, 'I tell you the truth, no one can see the kingdom of God unless he is born again' (John 3:3). Again, in John 3:5, Jesus said, 'I tell you the truth, no one can enter the kingdom of God unless he is born of water and the Spirit.' Thus regeneration is the initial, life-changing work of grace that brings a person to life spiritually, while adoption is the ongoing life-transforming work of grace that enables us to enjoy childlike intimacy with the Father.

Regeneration and adoption therefore need to be distinguished. A person is born again when they welcome Jesus into their lives by believing and trusting in the saving power of his name. When that happens, a person is given the right to become a child of God, born not of natural descent, nor of human decision, or of a husband's will but born of God (John 1:12). At the same time, believing in Jesus' name results in our receiving the Holy Spirit. The Holy Spirit makes real in our subjective experience the objective fact of our spiritual adoption. As the Spirit is poured into our hearts, so the 'Abba' cry pours out of our hearts. This cry is supremely the cry of the adopted child of God. Perhaps the best way to distinguish between regeneration and adoption is therefore as follows:

Regeneration occurs when the Spirit so quickens us that it can truly be said that Christ is in us. Adoption occurs when the Spirit so warms our hearts that it can truly be said that we are now in Christ (i.e. in the Son's intimate relationship with the Father). Thus, regeneration is about becoming a child. Adoption is the process by which we enter into that relationship of filial intimacy which Jesus enjoyed (and indeed enjoys) with God the Father.

ACKNOWLEDGMENTS

'Stay (Orphan's song)' by Brian Doerksen, copyright © 1995 Mercy/Vineyard Publishing. Administered by CopyCare, PO Box 77, Hailsham, BN27 3EF, UK. Used by permission.

Extract from 'How deep the Father's love for us' by Stuart Townend. Copyright © Kingsway's Thankyou Music, PO Box 75, Eastbourne, East Sussex, BN23 6NW, UK. Used by permission.

'Father God, I wonder (I will sing your praises)' by Ian Smale. Copyright © 1984 Kingsway's Thankyou Music, PO Box 75, Eastbourne, East Sussex, BN23 6NW, UK. Used by permission.

Extract taken from *Competent to Counsel* by Jay E. Adams. Copyright © 1970 by Jay E. Adams. Used by permission of Zondervan Publishing House.

Story of art collector's son first published in *Joy Magazine*. Used by permission.